TURNING POINTS

Defining Moments In The Lives Of NASCAR Superstars

by

Angela Skinner

DEDICATION

This book is dedicated to my two best friends: my husband, Mike Skinner, and my forever best buddy, Amy "Hoov" Plumley.

If any two people have taught me more about being a good person and achieving all I have the ability to achieve, it's been the two of you.

With your love and support I have more than most feel is attainable: TRUE FRIENDSHIP.

Angela Skinner

ACKNOWLEDGEMENTS

Many thanks to all of you in the NASCAR family who took time to share their personal "turning points" so that others might benefit from your experiences. Thanks also to Angela Skinner for providing these stories for us to enjoy. Her fine work and enthusiasm made this book a pleasure to produce. And a special thank you to Jackie Blair at Mike Skinner Enterprises. Without her hard work and dedication, this project would not have been possible.

This book is licensed by Mike Skinner Enterprises, Inc., and NASCAR®

Photo credits:

Chobat Racing Images: pages 51, 56-57, 61, 62 (bottom), 63, 64, 113 (bottom), 119 (bottom), 122, 125 (bottom), 162, 163 (bottom), 168, 175 (bottom) and 176.

CIA Stock Photography (www.ciastockphoto.com): pages 49, 50, 52, 53, 54, 55, 58, 59, 62 (top), 113 (top), 115, 116, 117, 118, 119 (top), 120, 121, 123, 124, 125 (top), 126, 127, 128, 161, 163 (top), 164 (bottom), 165, 166, 167, 169, 170-171, 172, 173, 174 and 175 (top).

Mike Skinner Enterprises: inside cover; pages 5, 164 (top).

Patrick Coyne, PhotosandFlicks.com: page 60.

Printed in the USA by R.R. Donnelley & Sons Company, Crawfordsville, Indiana.

Published by UMI Publications, Inc.
P.O. Box 30036
Charlotte, NC 28230-0036
www.umipub.com

UMI Staff: Publisher, Ivan Mothershead; Associate Publisher, Charlie Keiger; Vice President, Rick Peters; Controller, Lewis Patton; COO&VP and National Advertising Manager, Mark Cantey; National Advertising Sales, Paul Kaperonis; Managing Editor, Ward Woodbury; Associate Editor, Gary McCredie; Art Director, Brett Shippy; Senior Graphic Designer, Paul Bond; Graphic Designer, Mike McBride; Information Systems, Chris Devera; Administrative Staff: Stephanie Cook, Mary Flowe, Renee Wedvick

ISBN #0-943860-31-8

TABLE of CONTENTS

FOREWORD

by BENNY PARSONS

...

I wonder what it's like to be someone like Jeff Gordon. It appeared to me that from the time he can remember, he'd worked toward one thing: being a racecar driver. His hard work has paid off – probably beyond his wildest dreams.

I think most people are like me. As a teenager, I had no idea what I wanted to do with my life. In the spring and summer it was being a baseball player; in the fall I was going to be a football star. Once in awhile, I would attend a stock car race, so for the next week I dreamed of being a racecar driver.

For myself – and I think a lot of other people – there's that moment when you say, "yes, this is exactly what I want to do with my life."

I can't wait to start reading this book and see what that time was for a lot of my friends!

Benny Parsons
1973 NASCAR Winston Cup Series Champion

INTRODUCTION

by ANGELA SKINNER

...

Life lessons are an integral part in all of our lives. Most of us are so stubborn, that it takes a specific occurrence for us to learn and take one more step into a happy and near fulfilled life. I've always enjoyed talking to people, listening to how they make their lives more complete. Being upbeat and positive is a daily goal for me as well as an aid in my husband's career. I like for those around me to be influenced with my good intentions over my negative reactions.

I will say that living and traveling the NASCAR circuit is an emotional roller coaster. Just when you think you're on top, a simple cut tire can change your entire life and career. Learning how to cope and still enjoy the blessings of making it in NASCAR Winston Cup Series racing is the real life challenge. I've already learned a great deal about heartbreak and rejection in this business, but it wasn't until Pattie Petty, wife of NASCAR Winston Cup driver Kyle Petty, shared a few words before the start of a race at Pocono in 2002 that I learned a valuable life lesson. Since then, each day I live by the "Petty Scale" ... and here's why.

In 1999, I met my Prince Charming. I know it sounds hokey or right out of a Disney fairy tale, but from the first day I met my husband, Mike Skinner, I was deeply in love and in for more than a ride as a racer's wife. Mike was leading the NASCAR Winston Cup Series points in the spring of 1999. With a NASCAR Craftsman Truck Series championship and almost every non-points event won, Mike was on top of the world in racing. He had just signed a new three-year contract with premier NASCAR Winston Cup organization Richard Childress Racing and had the remarkable Larry McReynolds as his crew chief. A win had to be just around the corner.

Each weekend, the "31" team was a threat to win the pole and the race. The media labeled him as the best Cup driver without a win. Mike was due for his first points win week in and week out. He would drive his heart out to achieve his ultimate goal: a NASCAR Winston Cup points victory. We could taste the champagne from victory lane, but week in and week out, something would stand in the way: mechanical failure, getting wrecked by a lapped car while leading the race, tires blowing out. You name it, it happened. Before long, Mike was becoming the king of bad luck. Even newspaper artists began drawing cartoons of his misfortunes on the racetrack. Car owners and fellow competitors would come by to give their condolences and pep talks. We kept our heads high and continued to rally.

Three years later, three crew chiefs later, new sponsors and horrific crashes, the fight to win was still on; the fight to get the monkey off Mike's back and remove the dark black cloud over his career. The only problem was, although we were still fighting, car owners, sponsors and even fans seemed to give up on Mike Skinner. I'd had it. I allowed the pressure and the anxiety to eat me alive. I knew Mike was a winner, and I wanted every doubter to know it. The frustration was overwhelming, and it started to show on my face. I guess I didn't have that bubbly attitude and big smile one Sunday afternoon, because Pattie Petty noticed. As I walked with a scowl on my face, a light arm and hand wrapped around my shoulder and soul.

It was Pattie. She knew what I was feeling and all she said was, "I've been in this sport for over 20 years and it doesn't get any easier." All of a sudden I felt weak and ashamed for my self-pity. She continued to tell me how blessed we all are to be at this level and if I'd look at my problems on a scale, then maybe I'd realize life's not so bad. She told me to take my problems and rate them on a scale from 1 to 10. The key was 10 being the worst. If something goes wrong one day, then rate it. The funny thing is that one day you may rate a problem an eight, but one hour later it lessens to a five and the next morning it's down to a one. Coming from Pattie, a woman who'd seen so much tragedy in her life, including the loss of her own precious son in a racecar accident, put her outlook upon life into perspective.

I'll never forget the overwhelming feeling of love and comfort as I watched Pattie walk towards her husband's pit box. She was right. I felt silly and trivial for my emotions. I have a blessed life. I have a loving husband and wonderful family. I have a warm home and a hot meal anytime of the day. I realized I had to quit letting a NASCAR Winston Cup win determine my life. I believed nothing could be a 10 in my life. Pattie knew a 10, she'd lost a son, but there she was, continuing on and helping others who seemed beat down by the sport she and her husband knew so well. As I approached the #4 car pits, I took my seat upon the pit box, said a prayer and thanked God just to be healthy and alive.

After the race, Mike and I took a seat on our airplane. I gave him a huge hug and kiss and we sat back and relaxed, for we knew home was only an hour away. After 10 minutes in the air, our ears started popping. Even our dog, Opus, started shaking his head to stop the popping sensations going on between his ears. Our captain looked out from the cockpit to tell us we'd lost pressurization.

When a jet loses pressurization in the cabin, you lose your air source and breathable oxygen. You must land the airplane within five to 10 minutes or get back to a lower altitude before there is no air for the pilots and passengers to breathe. Supplemental oxygen is available, but it only has a short duration. If the pilots don't recognize the problem, then they could even pass out before realizing what took place. Professional PGA Golfer, Payne Stewart, along with his crew and friends, suffered these consequences and were sadly pronounced dead after their jet flew uncontrollably into the ground in 1999. I'd be lying to say I didn't panic inside. Mike held my hand tightly to calm my worries.

It wasn't very long and with God's blessing that our talented pilots landed us safely back at the Pocono airport. Race teams waiting to fly home all stared in disbelief, wondering why we had come back so quickly. They knew something went wrong. The first person I saw was Pattie. With a calm and warm smile she just asked how I rated the problem on a scale of 1 to 10. I laughed and said, "about a seven right now, but since we're alive and landed, it'll be a two tomorrow."

Over the past two years, I have collected many similar life challenges and lessons that your favorite NASCAR superstars have endured. Some talk about making it in their dream of stock car racing, others discuss how they cope in such a risky sport. Every story will give you some sort of motivation to live life and enjoy your own personal achievements and, hopefully, be a source of comfort in hard times. I hope you enjoy reading this collection of stories as much as I enjoyed interviewing and writing them. Maybe you too will learn a new life lesson in the process.

GREG
BIFFLE

"GETTING THE CALL"

...

O ver the months I spent working on this book, I realized one common denominator in most of the NASCAR drivers. They separated themselves from the competition in Late Model racing by making their dream happen and not waiting for some lucky opportunity. They are self-made men and dedicated all their time to racing. The other factor in this equation is their ability to separate business from pleasure and realize that hard work and no play can pay off eventually. This story has all the components, and the driver may surprise you. He's young, he's aggressive, and his ability to pull off professionalism paid big dividends and got him a call to the big leagues.

Driver Greg Biffle has one goal in mind these days: to win the NASCAR Winston Cup Series championship. He's already won the NASCAR Craftsman Truck Series and NASCAR Busch Series championships, so the Cup title would give him the only "hat trick" in NASCAR history.

Just a few years back, this phenom had a pretty simple goal in mind: just get noticed. Growing up in the Northwest made this dream a little difficult. Oval track racing was not a common weekend attraction in the state of Washington. The guys that did oval track racing had their own money, and the thought of a car owner and driver partnership was pretty unheard of. If you raced, you owned your own stuff and you drove for yourself. If you wanted to make it in NASCAR, you would have to move to North Carolina or make some pretty big impressions and allow your performance to sell yourself.

At the age of 19, Greg Biffle was a skilled welder. His parents owned a steel construction company, and as a result, Biffle acquired a tremendous fabricating background. Greg also had a wild side, and as a last-ditch effort to put their son on a more positive track, the Biffles convinced their son to put his welding and automotive skills to use by building a Street Stock racecar as a hobby. Greg had acquired a reputation – and many speeding tickets – as a teen, so his parents believed Street Stock racing could get their son off the streets. After visiting a few stock car and touring car races, Biffle caught the racing bug. He drove a couple of races and did pretty well, but the team he was with didn't have the money to be competitive. Biffle decided to return, but next time it would be with a car that he would build from the ground up. The finished results were beautiful, with craftsmanship that matched a Super Late Model racecar.

"I showed up at the racetrack, and people started to swarm around me and my car. They kept asking where I got the car. I told them all I built it. I built the roll cage and did everything; it really wasn't a big deal to me. I was proud of it, and I lost sixteen pounds building that car. I worked until three in the morning everyday to get it ready for that race."

Biffle quickly built a reputation for his craftsmanship and, at the end of the race season, found himself with a new business. At the age of 19, Greg Biffle started J&S Racing Products. There really wasn't a place for racers to buy car parts, so Greg began to build premium racecars for the very drivers he raced against. The only problem was that his customers had more money to race with than he did.

"Most of my customers would get four times the sponsor money that I would. I had five to ten thousand dollars a year to race with, and they were getting 30 to 50 thousand plus spare motors."

Not only was money Greg's downfall, but time also became an issue. He would work in his business building cars and selling racecar parts for other racers from 6:30 a.m. to 7 p.m., and then allow himself until 10 o'clock each night for his personal racing project.

"I kept my racing and my business separate. I also always tried to be professional in the way I conducted myself around the racetrack. I didn't go to the track looking like a bum in greasy clothes. I showed up professional with my shirt tucked in and tried to get the attention of someone who could provide me with a sponsor or financial backing."

Finally, in 1994, Greg took note of a new opportunity on the horizon. The Tucson Winter Heat Series quickly gained popularity, and it also caught the reputation of being a pool of undiscovered talent for NASCAR Winston Cup car owners. Dale Earnhardt discovered Ron Hornaday in its first season, and Biffle took notice. The series became the Superbowl of Super Late Model racers. Because it was an invitational event, it also gathered a huge draw of drivers from across the United States. To top it off, the Winter Heat Series was televised on TNN, and former NASCAR Winston Cup champion Benny Parsons commentated the event.

Greg watched the first year from home and gathered funding to race the event in 1995. With two Late Model track championships in the same year under his belt, Biffle headed to Tucson.

"I qualified fourth and won the first event. I then came back and qualified fourth and won again. In the third race of the Heat, I qualified eleventh and ended up second after we burned a plug wire. I won the championship and developed a relationship with Benny Parsons throughout that year's series."

The following year, Greg returned and once again did extremely well. Benny

Parsons felt Biffle had a fair amount of talent and, in Greg's words, became a salesman for his talent. Little did Greg know how much of a salesman. While Biffle was planning to take a year off from Late Model racing to build NASCAR Winston West cars, Benny was selling the Northwesterner to car owner Jack Roush.

Parsons was only passing through the Cup garage in Michigan when he innocently ran into Roush. Jack mentioned he was starting a third NASCAR Craftsman Truck Series team. Roush had planned to hire a driver from the Trans-Am Series, but couldn't agree on a contract. Benny then reminded Roush about that kid from the Northwest, Greg Biffle. Biffle was unaware of the conversation and continued his efforts to run NASCAR Winston West in 1997 in order to get more racing exposure at a different level.

One day, just minutes before noon, the phone rang at his race shop. Greg was known to talk on the phone a lot in his business. His clients wanted to speak with the man who owned the company, and his staff knew that if he took the phone call, lunch would be later than normal. Getting his shop foreman and partner, Roger Ueltschi, to quit working for lunch was also near impossible.

"I almost didn't take the call because I knew Roger was ready for our lunch break, but my parts manager yelled out that Geoff Smith was on line two. I thought it was kind of weird that they gave their first and last name, so I looked at Roger and told him I'd take the call real fast."

Roger looked at Greg with a disgusted face and went back to work. On the other end of the line was Geoff Smith, the president of Roush Racing. After his short introduction, Geoff told Greg that Jack Roush wanted him to drive in the NASCAR Craftsman Truck Series for him the following year.

"I was wondering at first if the call was real. He sounded sincere, so I didn't think it was one of my buddies screwing with me. Forty-five minutes later, I was still on the phone with Geoff. Roger kept motioning me to hurry. I held up a piece of paper where I wrote 'Roush Racing' in big print. He thought I was making up a story."

This all took place in 1997 just before the Labor Day weekend. By Monday, Biffle received another call from Roush Racing, and by Thursday, a contract was being faxed to Greg's attention.

"I hadn't even met anyone at Roush yet. I started reading the contract until I realized it really didn't matter what the contract said, and I turned to the last page, signed it and faxed it back."

In a matter of one week, Greg Biffle was ready to go truck racing. He had never tested, he'd never met with anyone at Roush Racing and he had signed a contract before he was ever face to face with Jack Roush. One recommendation got Greg Biffle into the NASCAR history books. He was serious about racing and saw an opportunity and went after it.

"I wasn't drinking beer and raising hell. I did have fun with my buddies at times, but it was away from the public. That call was like winning the lottery for me. I was driving a beat up old truck, eating Ramen Noodles and living in whatever I could find to live in - just in order to race."

Greg is sure that it was Benny Parsons' recommendation that got him the opportunity. He also reminded me that Benny's last recommendation was Ernie Irvan. Obviously, Jack took Benny's advice very highly. And obviously, Greg's long hours in the race shop, determination, and professionalism got him the call.

GEOFFREY
BODINE

"THE SURVIVOR"

• • •

Survivor. In my opinion, that pretty much describes Geoffrey Bodine. If you watched the inaugural NASCAR Craftsman Truck Series race at Daytona in February 2000, you would no doubt agree. That is also why, when Geoffrey told me that he was glad he had that horrific accident, I froze in disbelief. On a rainy afternoon in Darlington, South Carolina, I sat down to ask Geoffrey what life lesson he could share with me. I figured he would choose the Daytona crash, but the lesson was one that captured my attention.

"Up to the truck accident in 2000, I always thought in my career that I had been in some bad accidents and hit some walls, but I had never really been in 'The Bad One.' I really thought I would make it through my career without that bad wreck. I felt untouchable."

Geoffrey had no plans to originally run the Daytona truck race. He had just completed one year of a two-year contract with the #60 Power Team-sponsored NASCAR Winston Cup car. Geoffrey did, however, have plans for his son, Barry, to run four NASCAR Craftsman Truck Series races in 2000. Daytona was one of the four that the sponsor was interested in running. After many talks, everyone involved agreed that Geoffrey should probably run the race since he was more familiar with the track and had a good chance to win the race. He remembers the excitement of running that inaugural event. It was the first time trucks were to run Daytona, and they would not require restrictor plates.

"It appeared like it would be the way the Cup cars use to race Daytona, when we didn't have to have the plates and we had the old boxy cars. It was a lot of fun and there was lots of drafting."

That very race turned out to be the only event Geoffrey would qualify for that weekend. The NASCAR Winston Cup car did not turn a fast enough time to make the Daytona 500.

Race morning was nothing out of the ordinary for this driver – no strange feelings and nothing unusual. The one thought that never crossed Geoffrey's mind was the amount of rookies in the race. Most of the drivers in this series had never even seen the banks of Daytona.

"I didn't go into the race thinking, 'I gotta be careful with these guys.'"

The race began, and Geoffrey did get into a little trouble with a bent in fender. The new team pitted out of sequence and went to the back of the pack to regain position.

"Just before the accident, I told my crew not to worry, I was just being careful. The truck was plenty fast and I'll be cautious passing these guys. Obviously I wasn't cautious enough."

This veteran racecar driver knew to find a high line on the racetrack. By going high onto the fierce banks of this world famous track, Geoffrey could get a good run off the corner and down the straightaways to blow by his competitors. He was having fun until some drafting inexperience ended his day. Kurt Busch attempted to get into line through the trio-oval. On his attempt, he tapped another truck, which caused yet another driver to lose control – all right in front of Bodine.

"When I saw that happen, I just thought, 'Well, here I go into the wall and out of the race.' I started planning what I was going to do. Maybe get out of the truck and kick a tire. That was my usual way to get rid of my frustrations. I've never thrown my helmet because they cost too much."

What actually occurred was far from Geoffrey's post-wreck plan. The truck went airborne into the fence, tumbling over and over as pieces of this well-crafted machine blew apart. The large cables containing the fence did keep the truck from landing in the stands, but they also took part in chopping the truck to pieces.

"I thank God every day for that truck not going into the grandstands. I am also very thankful that those cables didn't chop me in half along with it, since it absolutely chewed the truck up. It cut the front end off, ripped the complete body off and cut the top of the roll cage. It was a miracle and the grace of God that I survived."

Safety workers quickly responded. "I remember hearing noise and thinking to myself; 'I am in Daytona. I was in a race. I was just in an accident.' And then I passed out again."

After cutting some pipes loose in the truck, a racecar driver's instinct came through. As soon as Geoffrey's legs were untrapped, he attempted to get out by himself.

"Some time later, one member of the safety crew told me I helped myself get out. I told him that's impossible. I was unconscious."

It is a racecar driver's pure and natural instinct telling them what to do when in a bad crash. That instinct can be so detailed it can push them to remove seatbelts, remove a helmet and get out of a burning car as quickly as possible – all while being semiconscious. This is an instinct that my own husband experienced far too many times, and he cannot explain or remember any of these actions. After Geoffrey unconsciously removed himself with the help of a rescue team, he showed a glimpse of life. As he lay on a stretcher wheeling toward an ambulance, his oxygen mask fell from his face. The survivor was actually reaching up to relocate the oxygen back to his mouth when cheers roared across the racetrack. It was a sign that told the racing world he had made it through the big wreck.

"I think that was the way God let me tell everyone I was alive."

The injured NASCAR Winston Cup superstar was then placed into the ambulance and rushed to a hospital. Doctors worked diligently over Geoffrey's body as he would gain and lose consciousness in the same minute. Once he was stable, the tests started.

"I still had not opened my eyes, yet I remember doctors preparing to move my body from the stretcher to a hospital bed. I actually told them to be real careful – that I was hurting really badly. And then they lifted me up on a three count and I passed out again."

It wasn't long after Geoffrey's arrival that many NASCAR drivers and their families began to gather in the waiting room to check on their fellow competitor. Bodine doesn't remember all his visitors, but one did stand out.

"Kyle, Pattie and Adam Petty came into my room. As they were leaving, Adam* put his hand on my shoulder and, in that Petty way, he said, 'Hey man, everything is going to be ok. If you need anything just call.' I remember that comment the most. Adam was a good kid."

To this day, Geoffrey still considers that accident unsurvivable.

"I shouldn't be here. I've been given another chance. I am sure of that."

As Geoffrey revealed his faith, he also revealed the special occurrence that took place because of his accident.

"My father had died four to five years before 2000. During my accident and my unconsciousness, my father appeared to me. He was very close and he smiled. I responded to his vision and told him, 'Dad I'm coming to see you.' He looked at me and said, 'No, it's not your time. There's more for you to do.' Then he disappeared. That was the first thing I told my family when I woke up."

It took a near-death experience to get Geoffrey to regain some faith and regroup on an old life lesson.

"I wouldn't change that day for anything. I really feel like God intervened and protected me during that accident. I feel like a pretty special guy because of that. I am very blessed."

Geoffrey overcame what appeared to be something unsurvivable. He could have dwelled on the bad luck. He could have felt sorry for himself, but instead, he decided to make a possible career-ending accident a blessing with his faith and a new saying.

"I no longer call the bad occurrences in life bad anymore. I call them tough. Whatever happens in your life, including the good and the tough, your faith will take the negative and make it a positive. That's your actual key to life. The tough survive because they don't give up."

Geoffrey ended our interview with a gleam in his eyes. He leaned toward me and said with happiness and boasting confidence, "I survived ... and I'm back!"

*In 2000, Adam Petty was lost in a NASCAR Busch Series practice session in New Hampshire.

3

JEFF
BURTON

"THE COMPETITIVE SPIRIT"

• • •

Being competitive is not just a key element in the heart of a racecar driver – it runs through their veins. But that competitive nature also means keeping emotions under control can be a real challenge. NASCAR Winston Cup Series driver Jeff Burton knows the good and bad of being too competitive. When he became a father, he learned a whole new aspect of that concept. Jeff Burton is a father of two. It took his daughter, Paige, to remind him of a little lesson about effort.

When Paige Burton was five years old, she came home pretty upset one after-noon when a competition at school didn't go the way she wanted. Jeff Burton knew he needed to sit his daughter down and teach her one of life's little lessons.

"Paige has my personality. She is very energetic and a little like a tomboy. She's not really competitive, but when she does something, she wants to do it well. I don't remember what it was that she had attempted to do at school that day, but she had not done too well at it and was pretty upset."

Knowing his own desire to always do well at any task, Burton sat his daugh-ter down to discuss putting forward one's best effort. He sat Paige down and asked if she had tried hard.

"She told me yes. Then I asked her if she enjoyed doing it? She answered yes again."

Jeff proceeded to put the two questions together and told his daughter that if she enjoyed what she was doing and had tried as hard as she could, then she had won. As Paige answered yes to all of his questions, her father then added it all up in one lesson that most parents try to teach their young children.

"The only thing we ask of you is that you try. When you put your best effort forward, we are content with that, so you need to be content with that too."

Paige understood what her father was saying and life went back to normal for the five-year-old.

A few weeks later, the NASCAR Winston Cup circuit was running at Pocono, Pennsylvania. Jeff Burton took his #99 Ford to second place. The car was supe-rior all day and, with Burton behind the wheel, looked like the car to win the race. Bobby Labonte held first position. With only 20 laps to go, Burton had run Labonte down to go for the lead. Third place was so far behind them that it was only a battle between Burton and Labonte. As Jeff went into the "Tunnel Turn," the transmission broke, the result of Burton trying to downshift too quickly. Worse yet, he didn't get the win or a second-place finish. Burton was unable to complete the race and ended up way in the back.

In the mad dash to beat the traffic out of the racetrack, Burton and his family started the second race of the day. When the race ends every weekend, all the drivers, crewmembers and their families race toward the airport. We frequently joke about who wins the race out of the track each weekend. One main reason to get to the airport quickly is to be first in the line of airplanes. If you end up 10th or higher in line, you could sit on the runway for an hour or more before taking off.

"In the mad dash to the airport, I had my family all lined out. Our motorhome driver had the kids on the golf cart already, and I was yelling out to Kim that she didn't have time to use the restroom. I took my place on the golf cart and began expressing how mad and disgusted I was about the race outcome."

As Jeff was convinced the world was coming to an end, Paige tapped her father on the shoulder. She then asked innocently, "Dad, did you try your best today?"

Jeff admits it was like a slap in the face.

"Here you are teaching your child to try her best, and then she has to ask me about the lesson I taught her. It was so good for me to hear her ask me that question. I didn't do my best because I had broken the transmission, but I was trying to do my best."

After Jeff caught his breath, he looked at Paige and told her yes. He also knew she was right. He didn't need to be so angry; he did all he could do that day in the race. Since that afternoon, Burton looks at effort in a new way.

"When things go wrong or not the way I wish, I ask myself, 'Did you put the effort in you should have put in? If you didn't have success, was it because you didn't put the effort in or was it because the effort you put in was the wrong effort?'"

As simple as it sounds, Jeff puts this lesson to the test often in his career and in his life. You can be upset if you put in the wrong effort; you should be really upset if you didn't put in any effort. Because we are human and competitive by nature, it's likely you'll be a little upset when things don't go your way. But understanding that your best effort was put forth can make you realize it'll all be ok. Effort really is a childhood lesson we all too often forget. It's good when someone is there to remind us. In Jeff Burton's case, it took his five-year-old.

4

KURT
BUSCH

"THE SPONGE"

...

When I sat down with NASCAR Winston Cup driver Kurt Busch, he promptly told me he really didn't have one single life lesson to share. He does, however, have many small lessons that he absorbs on a daily basis that made me realize why he was the youngest active driver on the NASCAR Winston Cup circuit and why he's seen so much success at the age of 24. Busch's ability to learn so quickly and develop professionally encouraged car owner Jack Roush to yank Busch from the NASCAR Craftsman Truck Series and throw him among the veterans on the NASCAR Winston Cup Series. Many critics felt Busch should have spent one year training in the NASCAR Busch Series, but in 2001, Kurt Busch took over the #97 car and surprised the world of NASCAR.

The first key element that has played a large part in Busch's racing success is simply his pure passion to drive a racecar. Growing up in Las Vegas, Kurt Busch caught the racing bug by going to the racetrack every Saturday night with his family. He was never really the kind of kid who was looking to find trouble or play a variety of sports; he just wanted to go racing.

"There were so many ways I could have gone. I played some little league baseball, but no matter what I did, I always ended up back at the track. The most unique story is how most every one of the drivers at the Winston Cup level had some obsession with cars at childhood. It was really just a way of life and all that I really knew."

That obsession got Kurt Busch to the professional level, but he did have to learn the other elements to be one of the best.

"I was pretty one-minded with just what I had to do with the racecar and what I needed to do to get that car around the racetrack. I knew how to build a racecar from the ground up, but I was so focused on what that racecar had to do for me that I didn't see much of the outside world."

Busch gives his car owner, Jack Roush, most of the credit for teaching him how to build a winning organization and attitude.

"It's almost like a thoroughbred horse. You've got your blinders on and you've been guided in a direction by your jockey, but all that horse knows how to do is run. You run at a pace you're comfortable with until you're told to move quicker or slower."

Once he began his rookie year, Kurt started to learn that there was more to becoming a champion than just knowing how to drive; you also had to learn the politics and the business side of the sport. Busch never really had someone to rein him back and teach him some of the business skills. His rookie year got off to a bit of a rocky start, not because of his ability as a driver, but his reactions to others on the racetrack. Busch felt his biggest challenge at the NASCAR Winston Cup level was being so young and not having the orientation of working within a professional atmosphere.

"I had to learn how to take all the lessons thrown at me and blend them into my personal style. I want to have fun and become more of a professional person about how I handle myself."

Busch did find that balance and, before he knew it, found himself in the winner's circle at Bristol Motor Speedway – one of the tracks where patience and focus is crucial. It was Kurt's 48th start in the series, and his willingness to adapt along with his desire to listen to those who had experience put him on the path toward a winning career.

"I think I became more of a team leader. This was something I didn't do my rookie year because there was so much I had to learn."

Busch began to get some of those rookie driver life lessons knocked out of the way. It seems many of us want to think we know all there is to know about our trade, when, if we would listen and learn on a daily basis, we, too, could improve our own professional careers and even our way of enjoying life. It is also easy to take in too much at once; before you know it you are focused on only one objective. Kurt's approach is pretty simple and his philosophy is ongoing on a daily basis.

"I like to grab different positive points from each and every individual I run into because every one of us has something different to offer. It's a matter of finding that lesson and realizing that it's your responsibility to make the right changes in your life and career."

Being a quick learner helped Kurt Busch find racing success at an early age. Maybe we all can take his simple advice and absorb a little something each day. You really can learn a life lesson every day if you open your mind to new things.

5

RICHARD
CHILDRESS

"WHEN OPPORTUNITY KNOCKS"

...

Richard Childress has seen success in three NASCAR racing divisions, winning six NASCAR Winston Cup championships with Dale Earnhardt, a NASCAR Busch Series championship with Kevin Harvick and a NASCAR Craftsman Truck Series championship with my husband, Mike Skinner. It's pretty ironic that this true-grit racer never wanted to be one of NASCAR's top team owners; he wanted to be one of NASCAR's top drivers. Fortunately, he recognized when opportunity came knocking, grabbed the door and entered into the history books.

I've always respected Richard Childress and felt rather proud that Mike had the opportunity to drive for him, but in 2001, he handed us a token that made me a little upset. I was honored that Richard thought enough to give us a gift, but its meaning indicated change. Mike and I had to learn a life lesson together to better understand the thought behind that gift from Richard. This story made me remember and better understand Richard's intention.

By 2001, Mike had not won a NASCAR Winston Cup points event in the #31 Lowe's machine. Richard had a lot of pressure to get the car into victory lane, and Mike felt the heat. The team would come close to a win, but the end result never found us celebrating with the trophy. We knew a change had to be made. I didn't realize Richard had been through a similar situation in his own career until we sat down to discuss one of his many turning points.

In 1981, Richard Childress was forced to make one of the hardest decisions in his life. Childress had been racing his own car since 1965, and even held a record for the most consecutive starts at 231. He was an independent racer without a solid sponsor, but he managed to pick up backing as he traveled from track to track.

During a hot Talladega evening, a meeting came about that changed Richard's career path for the better. Childress had put the word out that he would be interested in fielding a car for any driver who could bring a sponsorship. It was a casual announcement and one into which Richard hadn't put much thought. During a practice session at Talladega, Dale Earnhardt approached him with an offer. He would bring his sponsor, Wrangler, but Dale would drive the car, not Richard. Childress was used to running in the top-five regularly, but in 1981, his top-fives became top-20s, and that was a struggle.

"I knew I couldn't keep going, and I wasn't having as much fun. I let people know I'd do something different if the right opportunity came to me. Dale took me up on the offer."

Richard told Dale he would consider his offer over lunch. He immediately went over to Junior Johnson for advice. Johnson had seen great success, first as a driver, and then as a car owner, and Richard valued his opinion.

"Junior pretty much said there was a lot bigger need for good car owners than drivers. I knew I wasn't financially capable to continue as a driver/owner operation. I could see the possibility of solely being a car owner in the future of stock car racing."

That evening, Richard sat down with Earnhardt, representatives from RJR and Wrangler, and Phil Holmer from Goodyear in a hotel near Talladega, Alabama. There were only five people who put the deal together, a deal that would later bring Richard six NASCAR Winston Cup Series championships. It was also a deal that would take place quickly. Richard would step out of the car the following race in Michigan, and Dale would complete the 1981 race season with Childress as his car owner and Wrangler as his sponsor.

"I remember the race starting that day. I was standing there thinking, 'I'm only 38 years old; I'm not ready to quit.' But I knew I had to quit at the time because I could foresee the change in the sport. I was pretty nervous and just stood still and listened on the radio. I probably didn't say anything on the radio that day."

His friends joked that they were going to chain Richard to the pit box for the entire race just to keep him away from his car. They knew it was hard for him to give up. He'd been driving for so long it seemed unrealistic for the green flag to fall without him in the driver's seat. His vision for where the sport was going paid off in the end, and Childress learned that sometimes you have to change your way of life to see greater success.

"It was the best thing I ever did for my career and my life and family. It wasn't what I wanted to do, but I had to make a decision. When opportunity knocks and it feels right, don't let it pass you. I also proved to myself that I could do something other than just drive a racecar. The other lesson is no matter what you're doing, there's always something else you can do and do better."

That gift Richard presented to Mike and me was an inspirational book entitled "Who Moved My Cheese" by Spencer Johnson, M.D. Richard bought copies for all his drivers and managers at RCR just weeks before the 2001 Daytona 500. Little did we know that a major change was about to affect us all. Dale Earnhardt lost his life in the last lap of that race. In a sense, everything changed at RCR, and that's what the book presented using a simple parable about change.

Without giving up the entire story, "Cheese" is a metaphor for what you want to have in life – whether it is a good job, a loving relationship, money, possessions or health. In our case, the cheese represented Mike's job. Richard had presented the book to us earlier in that 2001 race season, just after the February Rockingham race. I felt Richard was letting us know that change could be near for Mike at RCR. He was also letting us know that he wished Mike great victories in his career path. Inside he wrote: 'To Mike and Angie, May your lives be filled with the greatest cheese.'

He was also being honest with Mike. Lowe's wanted to leave RCR, and Richard knew that the new sponsor for the #31 car wanted a younger driver. I remember reading one of the chapter outlines in the book that stated: "It is safer to search in the maze, than remain in a cheese-less situation." The characters in the book didn't want to see change and they did not improve their lifestyle by staying inside the same maze throughout the story. After reading the book, Mike knew that an opportunity was knocking for Richard and his race team. We both knew we needed to go elsewhere and look for a new racing situation.

Two years after receiving the gift and immediately after sitting down with Childress for this chapter interview, Richard's turning point reminded me to get that gift back out and read it again. I realized another way to look at the situation Richard had when he knew he needed to get out of the racecar and give Earnhardt a job. The book's author, Spencer Johnson, wrote: "Noticing small changes early helps adapt to the bigger changes that are to come." Richard made the right move in his racing maze; he ended up winning six championships with that new driver. Now he has eight NASCAR championships, over 100 wins and three full-time NASCAR Winston Cup teams along with two Busch Series teams. I would say he is enjoying a lot of good cheese!

STACY
COMPTON

"RISKING THE HOUSE"

...

Taking chances is a weekly occurrence in auto racing. Every time drivers climb into a racing machine they strap on safety belts and equipment to protect themselves in case a wreck occurs. Car owners take chances on new or veteran talents. Sponsors take chances by spending millions on the idea of signing with a winning organization. The list goes on and on, as it probably does in your life as well. I chose to add this chapter in my book because it's a story about taking chances, but more importantly, a risk that was full of heart and desire. Determination to do whatever it took to make it in the big leagues.

Stacy Compton had just celebrated a Late Model track championship at South Boston Speedway in 1995. With the love of racing in his blood, he began the next season with the same desire in mind, but the possibility to race in the NASCAR Winston Cup Series was always a recurring dream. He must have talked about this dream with many people, because one afternoon a man who had a small sponsorship on his Late Model operation approached him with a question that Stacy didn't take too seriously. The gentleman asked what it would take to get to the next level. Nonchalantly, Stacy explained that getting in front of the right people by running a NASCAR Busch Series race could probably help, but ideally, a NASCAR Winston Cup race. That was about the entire conversation, so Compton went back to working on his racecar and never gave it another thought. Three days later the man returned.

"He came back and said he'd bought a racecar! I asked him what type of Busch car he had purchased? He quickly answered that it was a Cup car. I yelled out, 'You did what?'"

Stacy had told him that you needed to get out in front of the right people and make it happen, but he didn't expect his friend to actually buy a NASCAR Winston Cup Series car. With the purchase made, Stacy began putting together what he called "some sort of a team" with his Late Model guys.

"We were taking a huge chance by hiring a bunch of Late Model guys with no Winston Cup experience, but the bigger risk would be monetarily."

Seeking financial backing was hard. Compton found a few companies willing to buy into the idea of running a Cup race, but in the end, he still came up short of funds. The team had set their sights on racing at Martinsville. The race was quickly approaching, and the only option became the bank.

"I needed a pretty substantial amount of money. I had raced Late Models and go-karts all my life, so I was known in my community. I walked into the bank, and they actually told me yes for the loan."

The bank gave Stacy the green flag, but they wanted some collateral before signing on the dotted line. They wanted his home, business and rental properties to secure the loan. The Late Model champion pondered the decision for a couple of days and finally convinced himself that his dream was worth putting his home up as collateral.

"I finally told myself that if I didn't take a chance like this, then I'd be running locally the rest of my life. There wasn't anything wrong with Late Models, but I wanted to get to Winston Cup."

With his hands shaking, Stacy walked into the bank and signed for the large loan.

"I was scared to death when I had to sign those papers. I kept thinking that this is the craziest thing I've ever done in my life."

Putting the stress of the loan behind him, Compton entered Martinsville, Virginia, to test a NASCAR Winston Cup stock car. Testing went well for the Virginia native and the media picked up on their success. Even racing legend Darrell Waltrip noticed the new talent.

"I was always a big Darrell Waltrip fan; he'd won so many races at Martinsville. I remember running Sterling Marlin down during practice and 'DW' came over to tell me we looked pretty good. He also told me I would burn up my brakes if I wasn't careful."

Compton had never run 500 miles. He had never been on radial tires and had never driven a race machine with more than 350 horsepower. Putting all this aside, he returned to Martinsville Speedway for the main event. He returned to the track and ran five laps of practice and posted the 25th-best time. The field of racers were only separated by half a second, and seven cars would go home. Stacy had to make the race on time, or return home to pay off a loan that would force him into near bankruptcy. As he walked down pit road to qualify, another racing legend ran up to Compton. Benny Parsons jabbed Stacy in the ribs and asked the new kid on the block if he was going to be present for qualifying.

"It sort of ticked me off, but I told him yes."

Stacy was calm as he prepared for the qualifying lap. He put on his helmet, tightened his seat belt and told himself it was just another day at the races. That was until he looked at the car waiting to qualify next. Dale Earnhardt was sitting in his famous black #3 Chevrolet right in front of Stacy.

"Big E pulled out onto the track and I all of sudden I thought, 'What am I doing here?' If my heart could have jumped out of my throat it would have."

Stacy quickly realized he had never been this nervous in his whole life. He knew borrowing such a huge amount of money just to make one NASCAR Winston Cup race was already crazy, but pulling out onto the racetrack right after Dale Earnhardt was simply nuts. Earnhardt ran a 20.39 on his second lap. Stacy knew it was a good time. As he looked out toward the scoreboard he saw the #3 in third place. Then Stacy took the green flag. He too ran a 20.39! His nervousness turned into happiness and relief as he knew he would make the show with that qualifying time. Not only would it make the show, but it also would put him in ninth position. At that time in NASCAR Winston Cup history, it made him the highest qualifying rookie ever in a NASCAR Winston Cup Series event. Then Benny Parsons came toward Stacy, running as hard as he could. Huffing and puffing, Benny said, "I guess you were here qualifying today!" Stacy looked at Benny with confidence and shook his head yes.

"It was a huge gamble. I'd never met Mike Wallace at the time, and even he walked up to me. He poked me in the chest and told me I didn't know him, but I didn't have a clue on what I had just accomplished. I believe that now because if I had not done that, I wouldn't be where I am today. There is no doubt in my mind."

Mike Wallace was right. Stacy Compton had made a name for himself, and he attracted some attention from the right people. The next year, Stacy found himself with a full NASCAR Craftsman Truck Series ride, which led him into both NASCAR Busch Series and Winston Cup rides as well.

"I was scared to death when I had to sign those loan papers. When we made that show in Martinsville, I didn't know if I'd ever find a ride or not, but after I made my first Winston Cup start, I thought it was worth every penny of it."

There really wasn't any defining moment that made Stacy's mind up to borrow the money. He just thought that you only live once. You have to take risks in life and you are taking a chance every time you wake up in the morning. The gamble paid off for Compton, but he did not actually pay off the loan until 2001. He raced three years in the NASCAR Craftsman Truck Series and two years in NASCAR Winston Cup before he was financially able to pay it off.

That afternoon race in Martinsville was a start for Compton in professional racing. He did stay on the lead lap until lap 283 out of 500. And as Darrell Waltrip had warned the rookie, his brakes began to burn up. The team came in, and Stacy, too, began to burn. As he climbed out of the car, he felt his body blistered from head to toe. The seat they had bought for the racecar was from another team and another driver, who was much smaller than Stacy's six-foot frame. Not aware of the construction of a seat for a Cup car, Stacy and his guys had cut out all of the insulation to where Stacy would be riding basically on the floorboard of the racecar. They didn't realize the padding and insulation in the seat was there for protection. The burns were so severe that it took two months to heal; even his shoulder blades were blistered. As Stacy put it, "I was cooked!" The boys from Lynchburg, Virginia, did get the brakes fixed enough to go back out and complete the race, but Stacy had to stay out of the car. His burns were too painful to continue. It was that same night when Stacy Compton learned another life lesson from one of his crew members.

"I looked at my guys and told then, 'Boys ... I can't get back in there.' One of the boys then looked at me and grinned to say, 'When you're dumb, you gotta be tough.'"

7

WALLY
DALLENBACH

"EVERYTHING HAPPENS
FOR A REASON"

• • •

I have a feeling that everyone who reads this chapter has heard the phrase, "everything happens for a reason." Sometimes you don't want to hear it, but hearing a story to back it up can change your feelings about a devastating experience in your life.

For me, getting fired from a radio station job that I dearly loved was the worst devastation I had faced in my career. I went directly to my best friend's house and, along with her comfort and encouragement, she spoke those words. I didn't want to hear it, but I had to believe it. You know what? She was right. If I had never been fired, I would have never moved on to a new opportunity in broadcasting, and I would have never met my husband. So whomever it was at that radio station that decided I needed the axe ... thank you!

NBC commentator and NASCAR driver Wally Dallenbach had a similar experience. Dallenbach refused to be beaten by the system, and he wound up with a pretty good job in the end.

"So here I was a week before the 2001 Daytona 500 in the beginning of my second year on a three-year contract, and I get a phone call saying we're out of money and we're shutting the doors. To say that was a very disappointing and traumatic phone call would be an understatement."

The Daytona 500 is the first race of the season and the biggest race of the year. Most drivers have their contracts in place months before, so Wally was pretty much without any options. He could not search for a new ride a week prior to the famed race. All the race teams were set, and if anyone was going make a driver change, it would not happen until two to three months after the season began. Wally suddenly found himself with a dilemma: He had made investments and planned the finances for his family thinking he had a three-year contract. All of a sudden, it all stopped.

"Unfortunately in this business, drivers find out that you are pretty much the only person you can count on. You have to have thick skin."

After a couple months, Wally began talking to race teams in search of a new driver, but they weren't the right opportunities.

"As a driver, you rely on all the people around you in order to succeed. You have to have great people behind you and great equipment to drive. I always drove racecars because I loved to do it. I was not going to get in another situation where I was a middle-of-the-pack driver. I wanted to be competitive."

Wally reached a new point in his decision making process. He would no longer drive for the money. He had to decide what was important to Wally.

He knew the difference in a winning race organization and one that was only semi-competitive. While driving for Hendrick Motorsports, he saw the possibility of winning and enjoyed the best season in his career. A sponsor change took that opportunity away and brought Wally to the race team that had to shut it's doors. Wally took the job with the underfunded race organization on a whim that a general manager from the Hendrick team could make a difference. But after Wally signed a three-year guaranteed contract, the general manager quit. Things went downhill, but Wally kept his commitment with the team and ran the 1999 season. After many disappointing performances, the team was without a sponsor. That led to the doors closing and the phone call that informed Wally he would not be in the Daytona 500. Frustrated and discouraged, he motivated himself to believe his misfortunes were for a reason.

"I told myself this is happening for a reason. I don't know what the reason is, but something is going to come out of this. I truly felt this, and through my career believed there was always something better."

While at home one day, the phone rang.

"My brother, Paul, called to tell me I should call Benny Parsons. NBC needed a third guy in the booth for the NASCAR Winston Cup broadcasts. He heard through the grapevine that they were having try-outs."

Shortly after that phone call, Wally found himself on a plane to Charlotte, North Carolina, for an audition. Without any television experience, Wally impressed the producers.

"I had always been on the front side of the camera being interviewed; it was a lot different being on the other side. NBC put me, Benny Parsons and Allen Bestwick in a little room, threw in a taped race and we fake-called a race from Michigan."

The producers were impressed with Wally's ability to not pull any punches. He said what he felt and held nothing back; they liked his edge. Two weeks passed before Wally was called for a second audition. That led to his offer to be on the NBC NASCAR team.

"When I started TV, it was difficult at first because I'm calling races and I'm talking about guys that I think I should be out there racing with. Now, three years later, I am much happier with my life. I am a better husband and father because I get to spend more time with my family, and I am just a happier person."

Dallenbach also began to see more racing opportunities. His success as a commentator brought offers to race in competitive equipment.

"I had more fun running the Busch races with Tommy Baldwin Racing and Pepsi in 2002 than I've had racing in a long time. My job with NBC opened up a lot more doors for my driving. They feel keeping me in a part-time race schedule is an advantage for their broadcast. If I'm on the racetrack on Saturday and then in the booth on Sunday, I can tell the viewers what the track conditions really are like. Anybody can go up and ask a driver what the racetrack is doing, but I was on the track, so I know firsthand. Nobody else in broadcasting has that credibility."

For Wally, his new career as a broadcaster works in his favor. He loves calling the races, and he'd much rather run 10 races in good equipment over running 35 events as lapped traffic. He is the happiest he's ever been, but he admits some days are still hard.

"There are times, like at Indy, it hurts to not be out there. That is a place I absolutely love, but I'll go to Martinsville and some other places I am not so fond of and say, 'Ha, ha, ha. I'm glad I'm not out there with those guys!'"

Maybe Wally got beat on the racetrack on Sundays, but he was determined to not be beat by the system. Believing all things happen for a reason gave him the encouragement to find his next opportunity.

"You can't tuck your tail between your legs and go away. In my case, I wasn't sitting by the phone waiting for it to ring. You have to make your opportunities and believe something better is in your future. In racing, out of sight equals out of mind. You cannot disappear because you are disposable. If you're not there, you'll be replaced."

Wally Dallenbach always wanted to leave this sport on his own terms. In my opinion, he is still in the driver's seat.

8

GAIL
DAVIS

"NEVER TOO OLD TO LEARN"

...

O n a brisk winter morning in the Ozark Mountains, a motorcycle enthusiast rides by in full biker gear. Onlookers noticed the sleek full-face helmet painted to match the bike, completing the look of biker perfection. What shocked the fans of this suave biker was what they saw when the helmet came off.

"I love to see the shock on people's faces whenever I pull off my helmet and there's this older woman with gray hair out on this crotch rocket. Going down the road, you just know they think it's a man."

Peoples' reactions make Gail Davis chuckle, but her love for riding a motor-cycle provides her with much joy. Along with husband Bill, Gail runs Bill Davis Racing, which fields the #22 and #23 cars in the NASCAR Winston Cup Series, as well as the #23 car in the NASCAR Busch Series. It's a common sight each race weekend to see Mrs. Davis perched atop one of her race team's pit boxes, so you probably wouldn't think riding a motorcycle would be such a stretch for her. What is a stretch about this story is the age Gail learned to ride a motorcycle.

The thrill of cruising on a motorcycle was a passion that Bill had enjoyed for many years. Gail had jumped on the back with her husband a couple times.

"I had ridden with Bill twice and was just sure I was going to die! Not that he was driving out of hand, but it was just foreign to me; and it was many years ago."

After her not so pleasurable experience, Gail left the riding to Bill and his buddies — until 1995. Kyle Petty had talked for a few years about gathering a group of people together to ride motorcycles across America and raise money for children. In 1995, his dream became a reality, and Bill made plans to join the first Kyle Petty Charity Ride across America after the race at Sonoma, California. Kyle's wife, Pattie, had encouraged Gail to come along for female companionship. Gail agreed, but she accepted to ride along in a motorcoach. The first day of the ride was cold and wintry outside. Gail sat warm and com-fortable inside the motorcoach.

"We were headed toward Newport Beach, and it really didn't look like some-thing I'd be interested in, but the next day was a different story."

It was a beautiful day in Newport Beach, and Gail took notice of three women riding their own motorcycles, one in particular.

"This woman rode up on a turquoise Harley Davidson. She was blonde and wore black suede fringed clothes. I thought to myself, 'WOW! She looks great.' That was a beautiful motorcycle and she acted like she could handle it."

The other attraction of this confident biker was that she was close to Gail's age.

With gorgeous weather and some inspiration from the other female bikers, Gail decided to ride along on the back of her husband's bike.

The plan was only to cruise for the first leg of the day's biking adventure, but from that day on, Gail ended up riding on the back of a bike for every leg of the journey. She even stayed with the group after Bill had to leave early for testing. Gail Davis was a newfound "biker chick" and jumped on someone else's motorcycle to complete the Petty ride in Charlotte.

"We had a huge time. I never realized people riding motorcycles could be so much fun. After the ride, I called Bill and told him I believed I could drive one of those things. So on my 50th birthday, Bill Davis gave me a motorcycle."

With a laugh, Gail then said, "That motorcycle sat in our race shop for a few months while I looked at it." It was a black-and-yellow BMW, and to Gail, it looked really big, really tall, and very heavy. Gail's birthday was in September. In February, she finally convinced herself to take a motorcycle safety course.

"We were using 250 Hondas for the course. They are much smaller than the bike Bill bought for me, and even balancing those was a challenge at first. The male instructor was sure I would never ride a bike. The female instructor was much more gracious."

After one month of getting over her first lesson, Gail took her first attempt on her own bike.

"For those of you who are old enough to remember Artie Shaw on the T.V. show 'Laugh-In' on his tricycle where he just turned over, that would have been me."

The minute Gail got on her bike, she just fell right over. With Bill's help, she picked up the motorcycle and continued to attempt getting back on. She dropped the bike a few more times, but she didn't quit. Gail Davis would drive this motorcycle.

"I'm sure I made a fool of myself that day, but it didn't bother me. I guess because of my age, I wasn't too humiliated. I told Bill I was sorry, but that bike was heavy and big. I had to remind him that he had his body weight to help maneuver."

Bill was pretty patient with Gail those first few attempts. Gail claims she probably still does embarrass him at times, but he is pretty proud of his wife. At the time of this interview, in April 2003, Gail had ridden 45,000 miles. She did admit that the first day she was supposed to ride solo, she prayed for rain so she wouldn't have to join the planned ride. Today, her greatest thrill is going fast and taking the curves. She'll also joke that starting and stopping still gets her.

"The reason I like to tell this story is because I hope to be an inspiration to other women who think they don't have the skills or they've never been interested in something or felt afraid they're going to hurt themselves. You really are never too old to learn."

It seems all too often we get caught up in not going after a goal because we don't want to make fools of ourselves, or we use age as a deterrent. Gail encouraged me to realize that people who limit themselves because they think they are too old or feel foolish are losing out on real living.

"My point is to try things. I've spent my whole life being afraid I was going to hurt myself. I didn't want to play sports because I felt I would injure myself and make a fool out of myself trying. Learning to ride a motorcycle at the age of 50 was a great confidence builder. I've seen some of the most beautiful parts of the country, and it's given my husband and me something truly in common that we love to do."

Gail will be the first to tell you that she isn't Miss Accomplished Motorcycle Rider, but the joy of learning something new and enjoyable has built her confidence. She now does more, goes harder and has no plans of slowing down because of age. In fact, she did have an accident on her motorcycle. She went too hard into a corner and ended up laying her bike onto the pavement. As Bill ran to her rescue, Gail was only worried about her bike. She was not scared anymore. In fact, she hoped the bike was in good enough shape to continue her ride.

With seven years of riding and over 45,000 miles under her belt, I would say Gail Davis is an accomplished motorcycle rider and, even more, an accomplished woman from whom we all can learn a valuable lesson: You really are never too old to learn. Not only can Gail ride solo now, but she can also ride across the entire United States by herself. And she promises to take the corners a little slower.

BARRY
DODSON

"TO SEE YOU SMILE"

...

L
egendary crew chief and now TV race analyst,
Barry Dodson, has seen tragedy in his racing
career, and has also faced the worst personal
tragedy any parent could imagine: losing both of his
children. But Barry doesn't want sympathy; he wants
to see you smile.

It's amazing to me how Barry Dodson can still laugh
and encourage others to be their best. Yes, he won a
NASCAR Winston Cup championship with driver
Rusty Wallace in 1989, and yes, he has won many races
in his career. He worked with some of NASCAR's greatest drivers, including Cale Yarborough, Richard Petty
and the late Tim Richmond.

Dodson came from a family of seven brothers and sisters. All graduated from high school but could not afford college. Barry went to work for Richard Petty after high school and learned a lot about racing early in his journey to one day be a crew chief. He was with Petty Enterprises for three championships and discovered that winning is all about people and preparation. He eventually worked his way into a crew chief position in 1985 with Blue Max Racing and driver Tim Richmond. They became a dominant force in the NASCAR Winston Cup Series. Tim Richmond was on his way to being a champion, but suffered from AIDS and passed away. Barry was devastated. Tim was his driver and, most important, a good friend.

Dodson regrouped and, with Rusty Wallace, won his NASCAR championship as a crew chief in 1989. Life was good for Barry. He and Rusty Wallace went their separate ways after their banner year. Barry went on to work with different racing outfits, including an attempt to own a race team.

In 1994, his life changed drastically. His two children, Trey and Tia, died in an automobile accident. Barry struggled after the devastating loss. Though he was still grieving, he needed to get back to work. Petty Enterprises offered Barry a consultant position for Kyle Petty's race team. The organization saw success immediately, and in 1995, Dodson took over as the crew chief. They ran well at Daytona, but a new engine program brought on some misfortune and their momentum was gone.

"I was in a free fall at that time of my life. I think you always are when tragedy happens. You never get settled in, and I was at that point."

Halfway into the 1995 season, Barry was exhausted, mentally and physically. Dover was the next race on the schedule.

"I've had a tremendous career racing, but that day in Dover, on my birthday in 1995, really made a mark on my life."

The team qualified poorly and, to add more pressure, Goodyear had changed the tires for the race. Nobody really knew what they were going to do or how to set up their cars with the new tires. After the last practice session, Barry told Kyle they had a pretty good car. They would have to come from 37th to win the race. Even with a glimmer of hope that they had a good car, Barry was still drained.

"I was so tired and exhausted. I told myself, 'I don't know how I'm going to make it to the end of the year.' With all that had happened in my personal life – and the racing wasn't good on top of all of that – and then it was supposed to rain the day of the race."

Prepared for a rain delay, Barry just laid on top of the pit box. He looked up to check the weather, and a cloud opened up. All of a sudden, there was a little sunshine. Barry looked at the glimmer of sunlight as a sign and took the moment to talk to his children.

"I looked up and said, 'Trey go get Tia and go find God. I need help.'"

Barry chose Trey to get his sister because Tia was always Daddy's little girl and always seemed to get what she wanted. He believed Tia would find God and tell him her dad was having a hard time.

"I'm having a real hard time guys, please help us run good today. We don't have to win, but we need to run good. It's not for me or my birthday, it's for y'all, and I love you."

The rain never came and the race started on time. That afternoon, Kyle Petty won from the 37th position. For 500 miles, the team never even made an adjustment to the car. Everything just kept happening right.

"I just kept looking up, and that rain went away. We kept getting stronger and stronger out on the racetrack. It was amazing."

They basically dominated the event, beating drivers who had been winning week in and week out.

"The thing that amazed me was that I know how much you have to change these race cars during the day just to stay on top of the racetrack. We never changed a thing on that car."

After the race, Barry was overcome with emotion. He grabbed his brother, who changed tires for the team, and told him about his prayer.

"I know in my heart that they heard me. It relieved some doubt that I had. It helped strengthen my beliefs and probably saved my life. I'll never, ever, ever do that again because I don't want to doubt what happened that day in Dover, Delaware. It was my biggest win. I know today that when I talk to them, they hear me."

The odds on Kyle Petty winning that race were probably 10,000:1. Pulling off the victory in such a dominant fashion made the win even more spectacular. Making no adjustment to the car was unheard of. In victory circle, Kyle Petty dedicated his win to Trey and Tia.

"I think about that day all the time. I don't feel sympathy or feel sorry for myself. A lot of people have had much worse happen to them. That day turned my life in a positive direction and I learned a lot about life."

Barry enjoys helping other people now, and he looks at other people's behaviors in a different manner.

"You see people standing in line complaining. People complain because they got a middle seat on an airplane and they can't find a place for their luggage. They are complaining about things that are insignificant in life. I just kind of chuckle about those people. These are the people that need a reminder, not to the magnitude that mine was."

That day in Dover proved to Barry that life is too short. He no longer accepts the highs and lows that life brings to him.

"After that day, I've found that it's no good to follow the valleys and peaks along our road in life. I put myself on the same level every day. The straighter and shorter line can eliminate the bumps. I like to see people smile, because it makes me smile. It's hard for me to smile on my own."

After hearing this story from Barry I felt shame, for I was one of those people who, just a week earlier, was complaining while standing in a line. His story did change my outlook on those aggravating moments in my life. I have never experienced the devastation that Barry had to encounter and overcome. I am not perfect, so I probably will catch myself complaining about something silly in the near future. But I will remember Barry's amazing moment, and I will try to crack at least a little smile. Someone else may need that smile too.

RAY
EVERNHAM

"NEVER QUIT"

...

NASCAR Winston Cup Series car owner Ray Evernham is a man of many talents. He was a racecar driver, a championship crew chief and a savvy team owner in NASCAR. He is also known to be driven toward perfection, meticulous, and takes racing very seriously. How he got to be one of our sport's greatest mentors is a story of pure tenacity: He never gave up.

Growing up in New Jersey, Evernham strived to be a racecar driver. He competed weekly at Wall Township Speedway, a third-mile asphalt raceway. With all his money invested in his racecar, Ray started to get a little frustrated with dismal results.

"We weren't doing good at all. I felt like maybe it was me and maybe I should quit, but I wanted to drive so bad."

A terrible crash in 1983 brought on a new perspective for Ray. He considered getting out of racing immediately. It would have been the perfect time to quit because the car was ruined and Ray had no more money left to race.

"I knew I shouldn't quit, and I actually went for the first time in my life and borrowed money to fix my car. When we were fixing the car, we put it into the frame jig and discovered that it was an inch short and the snout was crooked."

The discoveries gave Ray a positive outlook; maybe this was the reason he couldn't get a good finish.

Evernham and his crew worked around the clock fixing the racecar. They went back to Wall Speedway the next night and claimed victory. They continued to win, and Ray's stats proved him to be an up-and-comer in the NASCAR ranks. It also proved you can't quit.

"You never know how close you really are to making it if you really want to do something bad enough. I always look back at that day when we discovered the mistakes on that car. Whenever I think I am down and out, I think back to that time and say, 'There is a way out of this.' It's not the end, because that day could have been the end of my whole racing career. I almost gave up. I could have been selling used cars or working at a gas station in Jersey, but I wouldn't quit."

At the end of 1983, Ray nearly won the Wall Speedway track championship. That led to other opportunities in other racing machines. He ventured into IROC and played around with Modifides off and on until 1991.

"In 1991, I had the best opportunities that I could ever imagine in my life. I had all these great cars to drive in ARCA, midgets, and Modifieds. I was finally on my way."

With Ray's ambition set toward a professional driving career, another hard crash took him out of the drivers seat. Evernham was involved in an accident while racing at Flemington, N.J., but that didn't pull him away from racing.

"I know people were thinking, 'Oh, that poor guy ... that's the worst thing that could happen.' In reality, it was the best thing."

His devastation only fueled the fire. He would not quit! If he couldn't drive, he would be a crew chief. Evernham packed up and moved to Charlotte, North Carolina, in pursuit of being the best crew chief in stock car racing. He accomplished that goal winning numerous races and multiple championships with driver Jeff Gordon and Hendrick Motorsports. He left the stellar operation to create his own enterprise, Evernham Motorsports in 2000.

"I've continued that thought process from that one night of racing in 1983. If you stick to whatever you are trying to accomplish and are diligent enough, you're going to have some success. I continue to think that way even now with my own race teams. Right now, we aren't running as good as I think we should, but I won't quit. I know we can do this!"

I liked Ray's analogy on this topic. He tells his race team that not every basketball player can be Michael Jordan or every golfer be Tiger Woods or every racer be Dale Earnhardt, but you can be better.

It's encouragement that we all can use in any situation. Coming from such an honorable sports figure just makes it seem more possible. Too often we quit when we are really close to winning.

Greg Biffle's focus on professionalism has carried him all the way from the Late Model ranks to victory lane at Daytona International Speedway in July 2003.

Geoffrey Bodine's life-changing experience began with this accident during a NASCAR Craftsman Truck Series race at Daytona in 2001, an event that he now considers a "blessing."

In July 2003, more than two years after his accident, Bodine's enthusiasm for life – and infectious sense of humor – are more evident than ever.

No one has ever questioned Jeff Burton's intensity and competitive spirit, evidenced here as he prepares for 500 miles of tough competition.

Daughter Paige and wife Kim join Jeff Burton (top) to celebrate one of his four career victories at New Hampshire International Speedway. Burton remains a true student of the sport, working here with crew chief Paul Andrews.

Wide-eyed and ready to go, Kurt Busch brings into play all he has absorbed over his racing career and applies it toward becoming one the NASCAR Winston Cup Series' hottest young drivers.

Busch celebrates a big win at Michigan International Speedway in June 2003, the seventh win of his career 93 NASCAR Winston Cup Series starts for the 25-year-old driver.

Richard Childress' foresight into racing's future and willingness to change his personal career direction led to his joining forces with Dale Earnhardt, a decision that ultimately brought him six NASCAR Winston Cup Series championships as a car owner.

Stacy Compton put everything he had on the line to pursue his dream of becoming a big-league racer –
a gamble that paid off in spades.

As a driver, Wally Dallenbach was living his life-long dream – and couldn't have been happier. But circumstances bring change, and today, Wally is quite comfortable in his broadcasting shoes.

Accomplished biker Gail Davis enjoys a relaxing ride with good friends during the Kyle Petty Charity Ride Across America.

As a NASCAR Winston Cup Series team owner, Gail Davis is right at home atop a pit box, observing her race team's activities along pit road.

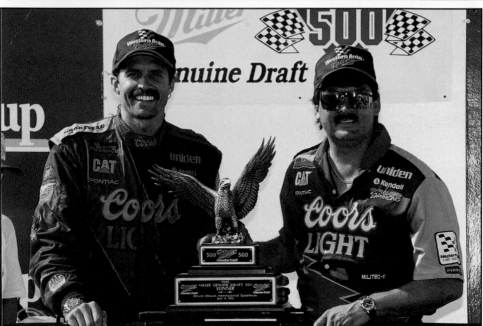

(Top) After cutting his racing teeth with organizations like Petty Enterprises, Barry Dodson (with jack) achieved crew chief status with driver Rusty Wallace. Together they won the 1989 NASCAR Winston Cup Series championship. (Bottom) Barry Dodson (right) and Kyle Petty celebrate a much needed – and very significant – victory at Dover in 1995.

Hard work and a "never give up" attitude has taken Ray Evernham from Saturday night Late Model driver to NASCAR Winston Cup Series team owner. Along the way, he picked up three NASCAR Winston Cup Series championships as a crew chief for driver Jeff Gordon.

Kyle and Pattie Petty in 1997. They taught me the "Petty Scale."

A.J. FOYT

"DRIVEN"

•••

A.J. Foyt – the only driver in racing history to win the Indy 500, the Daytona 500 and the 24 Hours of LeMans. He is the epitome of the most versatile driver in auto racing. I call that driven. His records are amazing with 35 consecutive starts in the Indianapolis 500, a race he won a record four times. He still owns the record as the only driver to have won seven national Indy car championships and the only driver to have won 67 Indy car races. Named Driver of the Century by the Associated Press, Foyt has 12 major driving championships. He raced sprint cars, stock cars, midgets and Indy cars, just to name a few. His statistics and versatility as a driver are still unmatched. What drove A.J. to become one of the greatest all-time drivers in history is simple.

"Growing up in Texas, I worked in my father's garage. He had worked on midget racecars all of his life. I basically decided to become a driver because I just hated to crawl under those cars in the wintertime when it was raining and throwing goop all in your face. I figured I would just try something else. I started by building my own modified Ford stock car."

While running midget and sprint car races, A.J. did dream about the Brickyard.

"I remember running down Georgetown Road looking at the Indy 500. I felt like, 'Man, if I ever get there, I will make it worth the wait.'"

Before A.J. could get to run the Indy 500, he first had to run a race at 16th Street Speedway. It was pretty much the biggest race of the year in the Midwest for up-and-comers. Foyt left home with a midget car and only $200 in his pocket. He didn't have any of the fancy tires like his competitors, but he was driven.

"I'm sitting there with about 150 midget cars on the entry list. Only 30 would qualify for the races. They ran three complete races and I qualified for the biggest event."

As if A.J. wasn't driven enough, a visit from a famous Indy car driver left him with a moment he would never forget.

"One of my funniest stories and one which really turned my attitude around was when Jimmy Reese came to visit me just before my race. Jimmy and his buddies would usually come over to watch the 16th Street race to mess with all of us before our main event. They would run the Indy 500 the next day, so they were the big-time racers and we were the wannabes. I was changing weight on my car and he came up to tell me that I didn't have a big enough right-front tire. I replied that I understood that, but I didn't have any money and I had to run what I brought."

As A.J. began to change the cross weight on his racecar, Jimmy told him he had one problem.

"He told me I needed to jack the weight on the right side just right ahead of the stand gear."

Now, if you are confused with that comment, don't feel alone because A.J. looked at Jimmy with a look of mass confusion on his face. He looked up at

Jimmy and yelled out, "What are you talking about?" Jimmy replied with laughter and said, "That throttle foot, jack a little more weight there." A.J. thought about Jimmy's comment and replied, "Okay, that's a good point." Later that year, Jimmy Reese lost his life in a racecar, but Foyt always remembered his encounter with the driver.

A.J. went on to enjoy all types of racing and won his first championships in sports car and midget divisions. He continued to run in different racing divisions and became the only driver to also win 20 USAC races in one year. That year was 1961, and Foyt won 10 midget, 6 sprint and 4 Indy car races. He had the ability to adapt to change and win. He wanted the Daytona 500, but in order to run it, he needed the correct amount of FIA points – a prerequisite for stock car racing's main event. The FIA is a national automobile competition committee. You must be a member and meet their standards before you can qualify for NASCAR competition.

After Foyt ran a factory Pontiac in USAC and won the Indianapolis 500, he finally qualified to run the high banks of Daytona. A.J. would run every NASCAR race he could enter, but he was limited to only full FIA International events. In 1972, Foyt captured the Daytona 500 trophy. He still remains today as the only driver to win racing's triple crown: The Indy 500, The Daytona 500 and 24 Hours at LeMans.

He only ran 128 NASCAR events, but won seven of them and captured nine pole positions. Renowned for his Indy car prowess, Foyt still carries a lot of clout in the NASCAR Winston Cup garage. Today he has one current NASCAR Winston Cup driver who is after his record of being the most versatile driver in history. After Tony Stewart won his NASCAR Winston Cup championship in 2002, he called Foyt. A.J. was in Charlotte and had intentions of calling Stewart to congratulate the new NASCAR champion, but Tony beat him to it.

"Tony was still in Homestead to test his racecar the following day. When I answered the phone, he immediately said there was something he wanted to tell me. I asked what it was and he starting laughing and exclaimed, 'I've done something you haven't! I won the NASCAR Winston Cup Series championship.'"

A.J. fired right back, "Well Tony, I never tried. It probably would have been easy if I wanted to, but you know what? I won the Daytona 500, the Pepsi 400, the 125s at Daytona, and I also won the Indianapolis 500 four times. Have you ever done that?"

Tony started to laugh, and that was the end of the phone call.

When I asked Foyt to describe his unique talent and ability to adapt to any racecar, his answer was simple: "I just thrived on winning. If I got beat, I felt like the world was coming to an end. I wasn't realizing how many races I'd won in different categories until later on. I basically just concentrated one hundred percent. I was driven."

Today A.J. Foyt owns his own NASCAR Winston Cup and Indy Car operations. He retired as a driver from Indy cars in 1993 and completed his NASCAR career in 1994 at the inaugural Brickyard 400 in Indianapolis. Despite all of his driving achievements, Foyt believes there are still more goals to accomplish. He wants to visit NASCAR's victory lane once again, but this time as a car owner. It's a place he's been before and is driven to visit again.

BETTY JANE
FRANCE

"ONE MOMENT IN TIME"

...

O ne thing I've enjoyed throughout my time spent
on the NASCAR circuit is the amount of friend-
ly and welcoming people I've met. Betty Jane
France is probably the most inviting. Betty Jane is the
wife of NASCAR Chairman of the Board Bill France Jr.
Her charm and warm personality make you proud to be
a part of the sport she and her husband oversee. Her
dedication to NASCAR and children's charities make her
a role model for both men and women.

After spending a little over two seasons with my husband on the NASCAR Winston Cup circuit, I decided I wanted to meet the first lady of NASCAR. On a Monday morning in Daytona Beach, I called the NASCAR corporate offices and asked for Mrs. Betty Jane France. In all reality, I thought I would be given the cold shoulder and a computer messaging system to leave a voice mail, but I was determined that I had to try. To my surprise, a very polite lady answered the phone. I almost froze! Then I caught by breath and said, "This is Angela Skinner and I would like to ask Betty Jane to join me for a lunch this week." I paused and thought, "Well, I am sure they will think I'm nuts to just call someone I don't know and invite them to lunch." But I was told that Mrs. France would probably love to have lunch. A couple of hours later, the date and time were set and I had a lunch date.

It probably wasn't until the day of the luncheon that I panicked. I don't know why, but I felt I would not know what to say, or I would make a fool of myself. What if I take a drink of my water and a large ice cube falls onto my lap and I end up with water all over myself? What if I say the wrong thing and she ends up thinking I am an awful wife for Mike? Trust me, I thought up every snafu that could happen when you are nervous about meeting someone for the first time. I even called up Linda Helton, wife of NASCAR President Mike Helton, for emotional support.

When I arrived at the restaurant (after trying on five different outfits for what I thought was the most suitable) I sat at the table waiting for the big meeting. Within minutes, I caught a glimpse of a beautiful lady with a stunning smile approaching the table. Immediately I knew she was down to earth and I didn't need to worry anymore. She introduced herself, and I don't think we stopped talking for two hours. When the check came at the end of our meal, I quickly went to grab it. Betty Jane was quicker and took the bill to pay. Humiliated that I had invited her, I asked if I could please pay since we were there on my invitation. Betty Jane gave me a witty smile and said, "You better let me pay. I'm pretty stubborn and I like to get my way."

We laugh now about what a big deal I made of the lunch date, but I must admit I am still honored each time I get the chance to sit down with this remarkable lady. When I asked her if I could include her in my book, I learned something new about Betty Jane; she too loved to write. She asked if she could write her own chapter. The following is one of her life lessons:

Life has many turning points, much like a curve in the road. If we had a way of knowing what was around the curve, we may choose not to go there.

Bill and I had made arrangements for a trip to San Francisco to meet with some great friends of ours in what promised to be a wonderful trip. We awoke on the morning of October 17, 1989, ready for the day. I met my friend for shopping around 10:00 a.m. We had a great morning, a feastful lunch and decided to continue our shopping. My friend had spent all of her life in San Francisco and knew the city like the back of her hand. We had both remarked the day was unusually warm for San Francisco, but it certainly did not slow us in our quest for more shopping.

We were in Neiman-Marcus and at 5:04 p.m., the lights began to dim and the chandeliers were swinging in a haunting way. Then the loud rumbling began. We rushed into a doorway where we stood in horror and shock until the quiet set in. We feared the floors above would give way and we would never survive. Finally, someone escorted us down the fire stairs and onto the street where people seemed to be in shock. Traffic was at a complete standstill and glass covered the sidewalks from the shattered windows. Homeless people slept quietly in the park as we made our way through and climbed to Knob Hill, hoping our hotel had survived. As we neared the top of the hill, we could see our hotel and our husbands, who were waiting outside because the hotel had been evacuated. I breathed a sigh of relief; we had survived an earthquake which measured 7.01 on the Richter scale. Somehow, that one moment in time changed my perspective on life forever. Seize the moment; we are promised no tomorrow. Life is a beautiful gift to be cherished.

BILL
FRANCE JR.

"A NICKEL & DIME LESSON"

...

I n the late 1950s, William Henry Getty France decided to build on a dream. The racing community refered to him as "Big Bill," and Big Bill had seen pretty big success on the beach courses in Daytona. NASCAR was in its infancy and France Sr. knew he needed to expand the sport. The beach was becoming too bumpy and rutted for the modern, faster stock cars in development. Grandstands at the beach could no longer hold the growing number of race fans, so France Sr. turned his vision of a high-speed and banked racetrack into a reality. The Daytona International Speedway would be modeled to rival the world famous circuits at Indianapolis and Le Mans. Daytona would also host the most prestigious NASCAR event: The Daytona 500.

In January 1955, France Sr. began his bids for approval on his new vision. By October 1956, all approvals were met, and the France family had a lease with the Speedway District for 377 acres to build their race facility. After the financial and city approval hurdles were cleared, bulldozers began clearing land near the Daytona Beach Airport to make way for "The World Center of Racing."

It was now 1957, and Big Bill used some old fashioned methods to get his racetrack complete for the first running of the Daytona 500 by February 1959. His son, Bill France Jr., ran a grader, bulldozer and compactor for 13 months, 7 days a week, 10 to 11 hours a day. It was during this time that France Jr. learned a pretty valuable lesson in the world of business.

Bill Jr. decided to be helpful toward the heavy equipment operators one afternoon. It was a hot and humid Daytona day so Bill carried a cup of water from his own truck to a specific bulldozer operator. The bulldozer was sinking in mud and the operator was hard at work.

"I hollered at him, 'Here is some water,' but he wouldn't get off the bulldozer. I thought to myself that he must not need the water so to hell with him."

About that time, Bill Sr. approached his son. "I know it's not good that he won't come and get that water from you, but it's obvious that he's not coming down off that bulldozer." Bill Jr. angrily replied, "If he wants some water, he'll have to come over here." Then Bill's father taught his son a lesson in management.

"My father gave me a stern no. He told me I would go and give that man his water because while we were arguing over pride, that particular machine had stopped working. The track had to be completed by February, and keeping the machines operating was what was important. Don't worry about that water."

The next thing Bill knew, he was carrying that water over to that bulldozer operator. It was aggravating to Bill Jr., but he learned from such a simple incident that nothing was happening to complete that track if he argued with the workers.

"The point of the story was that a lot of times you have to do things you don't want to do. Many times it's someone else's responsibility, but you've got to keep your eye on the ball and see the big objective. The big objective is what's important. It was a nickel and dime lesson, but key for me to learn. I've had a number of those experiences in my life, and they all helped my success."

After two years of construction, Daytona International Speedway debuted its first event with the running of the 1959 Daytona 500 on February 22. The race lasted 3 hours, 44 minutes and 22 seconds. Richard Petty won by an estimated 18 inches. The Frances reached their goal, and Bill Jr. learned a few lessons throughout the process. They may have been nickel and dime lessons that Bill's father passed on to his son. I call it street smarts, and the France family has a lot of it. Most of the time, it's those simple lessons that make you the most successful. In Bill France's case, you'd have to agree.

KEVIN
HARVICK

"IN ONE INSTANCE"

...

In February 2001, Kevin Harvick had two
season goals. First was to win the NASCAR
Busch Series championship, the other was
to run seven NASCAR Winston Cup Series races
with new sponsor AOL. He did capture the 2001
NASCAR Busch Series championship, but the
NASCAR Winston Cup agenda all changed with
one instance.

Kevin's career was strategically planned with AOL firmly established as his sponsor.

"The plan was originally to drive Dale Earnhardt's car at Richard Childress Racing five years down the road, but everything happened so quickly because one afternoon Dale told Richard, 'If you don't hire him to run Winston Cup, I'm going to.' Richard found AOL to sponsor my Cup car. I planned to go and learn as much as I could from the '3' and '31' teams. I felt I could use the seven races as a mentor program so I would not have to go through all of the bad occurrences and all the mistakes that take place in your rookie year in Winston Cup"

There was also one other personal plan on Kevin's 2001 calendar: he would marry fiancée DeLana Linville prior to the Las Vegas race. With his personal and professional life in full gear, Harvick traveled to Daytona to run the first race in the NASCAR Busch Series season. He completed the race with an impressive second-place finish. Immediately after the race, Harvick left for home to watch the Daytona 500 in his own living room. Kevin and DeLana watched the race, but turned off the television when the broadcast was completed.

"We just figured like everyone else that Earnhardt had wrecked and it was no big deal. Everything will be fine. We will go on out to dinner and go to the shop tomorrow to see how tore up the car is because Dale is fine. Every other time he's been fine and even if he is hurt, he'll get back in the car and drive next week. Little did we know that one instance would change everything."

As Kevin and his soon-to-be wife left for dinner, DeLana picked up her cell phone to call Dale Earnhardt Jr.'s public relations manager. She, herself, worked in PR representing Randy LaJoie and felt it important to check on the situation. She did not get a positive response from her phone call. Shortly after, Todd Berrier, who was Kevin's NASCAR Busch Series crew chief, requested his and DeLana's presence at the home of Mike Dillon. (Dillon was Kevin's team-mate in the NASCAR Busch Series and Richard Childress' son-in-law.) It was there that Harvick learned of Dale Earnhardt's death.

"Everyone was a wreck at Dillon's house. We all tried to figure out where

Richard Childress Racing was going to go as a whole. That event affected two Winston Cup teams and two Busch teams. We felt Richard would say, 'I'm done, I don't want to race anymore.'"

Everyone at RCR, including Kevin, waited to hear from Richard Childress.

Still in Daytona, Richard sent word that everyone would still have their jobs, all teams would race in Rockingham, and the AOL team would still test in Atlanta. Kevin recalled it being very tough to carry out all the normal things that you are supposed to do in a test. RCR closed the racetrack to the media to help the team concentrate on the task at hand.

Around 9 p.m. Wednesday evening, a call came for Kevin from Richard. He was asked to report to the race shop. Kevin drove alone to RCR. When he arrived, Richard, Bobby Hutchens and Kevin Hamlin (the crew chief for the #3 car) were waiting.

"I walked into Richard's office and he immediately said, 'We want you to drive Dale's car. It's an awful big undertaking, but we think you can do it; will you do it?' I agreed, but I did tell them I did not want to drive a black car and I did not want the number to be 3. Richard had already planned for the same, and we went to Rockingham with a white-and-black #29 Chevrolet."

At this point, most people felt Kevin would drop his NASCAR Busch Series championship dream and focus only on the NASCAR Winston Cup Series. Instead, this aggressive driver decided to continue the quest in the NASCAR Busch Series and attempt to gain NASCAR Winston Cup Raybestos Rookie of the Year status all in the same season! The new plan would start the very next day in Rockingham.

"I wasn't really nervous at that point; it was like helping one of your friends. I didn't ask any questions that evening in Richard's office. Richard asked me to drive and that's what I felt I needed to do. It also wasn't just Richard asking, it was two hundred RCR employees depending on someone to have those race-cars back on the track."

For Kevin Harvick, it took that meeting and the most devastating tragedy in NASCAR history to realize firsthand that everyone is vulnerable at any given moment. You never know what's around the corner in your life, and taking every precaution can't be taken for granted.

"That instance has taught me more than anything else in life. Take every precaution that you can. Not just in a racecar, but in your home, in your car and with your loved ones. Don't be lazy about the little things. Before that night, I felt I could hit anything and anybody in a racecar. I had such tunnel vision that anything around me could not be hurt, and if I wrecked, it would never be a big deal. That wasn't the case anymore."

Kevin appeared in Rockingham with a new approach. Before he climbed into his #2 NASCAR Busch Series car and his #29 NASCAR Winston Cup car, he strapped on a head-and-neck safety restraint for the first time in his racing career. The seat belts were looked over with more detail and the process for improvements in his seat were implemented.

His ultimate plan for the 2001 season had changed, but he ended it with more than one racing title. At the end of the season, Kevin Harvick walked onto a stage in New York City as the 2001 NASCAR Winston Cup Raybestos Rookie of the Year in December. In January, he walked onto a stage in Los Angeles as the NASCAR Busch Series champion.

15

MIKE
HELTON

"RELATIONSHIPS"

...

Most fans of racing don't get the opportunity to walk around in the NASCAR Winston Cup garage. Most fans of racing don't get to see NASCAR President Mike Helton walk his office grounds with stern authority each weekend on the circuit. They also don't get to see the respect every single person in NASCAR – drivers included – have for the man in charge of NASCAR racing. Though the drivers and crewmembers know Mike Helton can determine your entry into the garage area, they also know the smooth side of Mike Helton – the caring and concerned man who loves his job and the people whom make his job possible. He knows the value of relationships.

"In racing, you learn really quick that there's not one relationship, there's a whole host of relationships. Every action with one relationship is going to have a cause and effect on your other relationships," Helton says.

When I first started attending races with my husband, Mike Skinner, I discovered the powers of Mr. Helton and the importance of relationships. When you walk into the NASCAR Winston Cup garage, there are a few rules by which you must abide. One is that you must wear long pants and no sleeveless shirts. The second is that you must wear closed-toed shoes.

Being the female that I am, I decided one Sunday morning that I would rebel against the rules and wear a new pair of open-toed sandals. I entered the garage area and headed toward the church service when I was promptly approached by Mike Helton. I was new in the garage and Mike was sure to welcome me into his weekend office. As he hunched down to give me a hug he whispered into my ear, "nice shoes." I knew right away that I was caught.

I went into the weekend church service and told Mike about my greeting from Helton. Needless to say, I returned to our motorcoach and changed into a "legal" pair of shoes before taking in the race from the pits that afternoon. I ran into Mike Helton prior the race and made sure I pointed out my closed-toed shoes. He grinned and patted me on the back, telling me he was just giving me a hard time, but I knew he was letting me know to abide by the rules. He just knew how to make me feel better. He was pleased, and I was pleased that I was no longer in trouble. From that day on, I had a new relationship with Mr. Helton and a newfound respect.

When I sat down to talk to Mr. Helton, I learned that his most important career decision was based on a good relationship and that the chain reaction that followed allowed him to become what he is today.

Growing up, Helton had a passion for racing. Mike was born and raised in Bristol, Tennessee. Volunteering at Bristol Motor Speedway was a rush for the young racing fan. He did attempt to drive dirt tracks as a young man and discovered he would probably never be a driver. In order to remain close to the sport, he'd hang out at every race he could attend and help out in any way needed.

"Back then it was a whole different ballgame. The tracks depended on volunteers and a whole lot of temporary help."

His persistence paid off in 1980 when he received his first full-time job in racing as a public relations director at Atlanta Raceway. For a long time in Atlanta, Helton enjoyed his position and was very content. The staff was only made up of five people, including Mike.

"It was not unusual for me to spend a half day in downtown Atlanta talking with sponsors and then cut back to the track, change clothes and paint the walls in the late afternoon. Everybody did a lot of different jobs. I really liked that; it was like running a farm."

Eventually, Helton was running the racetrack, but as the sport of auto racing began to change, so did the environment at Atlanta Raceway. Helton became frustrated and was ready to give up on motorsports altogether. He already made his decision to take a job with a private company in downtown Atlanta that had nothing to do with racing.

"I was nearly ready to walk right out of the sport, but one conversation brought me back in a big way."

In November 1985, before the race weekend started, Helton asked Jim Hunter and Les Richter to meet him in his office at the racetrack. At the time, Hunter and Richter were the representatives from NASCAR on the racetrack operations side.

"I sat them down and explained to them that the weekend's race in Atlanta would be my last because I felt I needed to move on. Les and Jim asked me if it was really what I wanted to do. I told them no, but I really didn't see any other promising opportunities."

Though Mike had received numerous offers to work in other forms of motorsports, none seemed better than what he was doing at Atlanta.

Helton went on and got the race weekend started and completed. By Tuesday morning, his phone was ringing. It was Les Richter wanting to know if Mike was absolutely sure he wanted to leave racing. Once again, Helton explained that he really didn't want to leave the sport, but did not see a better future for himself. Then Richter asked Mike if he wanted to come work at Daytona. By May 1986,

Mike and his wife, Linda, were moving south to Daytona Beach to work for International Speedway Corporation, the corporate parent of Daytona International Speedway. It changed everything.

"I went from running Daytona in May of 1986 to Talladega Speedway in October of 1987, and then onto NASCAR to be the vice president of competition."

The key thing that opened Mike's eyes to pursue a career with NASCAR was their commitment.

"NASCAR and ISC were the only outfits in the motorsports business that lived, ate and drank the racing business. In that era, many racetrack owners were in racing for a hobby. The France family got up in the morning thinking about racing. They went to bed at night thinking about racing. There was no distraction. If they were making a future out of the sport and their careers depended on the sport, then that would be a pretty neat place to make a career for myself."

He has definitely made a career for himself and still loves the business and the people in racing. The power of a positive relationship changed Mike Helton's entire career path. His ability to be patient and let the chain reaction occur put him in charge and on top.

16

PHIL
HOLMER

"DOING GOOD FOR OTHERS"

. . .

You may not know who Phil Holmer is, but if it hadn't been for his simple act of kindness many years ago, the union of NASCAR car owner Richard Childress and legendary driver Dale Earnhardt may have never taken place. Phil is the marketing manager for Goodyear Racing. He keeps race teams' tire budgets and suggestions for the best racing tire in perspective. Holmer has been a regular in the NASCAR garage since 1976, but he began his career as a sportswriter. His ability to eloquently cover racing led to a job with NASCAR, but he really wanted to just write about football.

"In the 1960s, the youngest and newest guy got stuck with covering what we called the 'Three Rs' (racing, rodeo and 'rastling'). The older more experienced guys got to cover football and basketball. I enjoyed going to Daytona and covering Speedweeks and the Daytona 500. Bill France Sr., the founder of NASCAR , liked my work and offered me a job in public relations."

Holmer took the opportunity with enthusiasm and worked for the racetrack for nine years. Then another adventure arose. Goodyear tire company became the official tire company for the NASCAR Winston Cup series. They wanted Phil to join their company and work in their racing division; he accepted. In his second year with Goodyear, Phil helped put together a deal that would change the NASCAR history books. The deal took place in a hotel in downtown Anniston, Alabama. Tired crewmembers and drivers were enjoying happy hour after a long day practicing for the Talladega race. Phil was minding his own business when someone approached him and told him he was needed in room 2.

"I remember it was around 7 p.m. I knocked on the door wondering what in the world was this impromptu meeting all about. Richard Childress answered."

The room was dark. It was a suite with a living room off to one side, and on the right corner sat a little wet bar. All of the lights were off in the room except for the bar. Childress sat Phil down at the lit bar.

"I was kind of looking around and sneaked a peak over my shoulder. I thought to myself, 'I think I can see people on the couch.' To this day I remember those images."

Masked by the darkness, Phil knew there were three bodies in the background. They never spoke a word. Richard and a representative from Wrangler began the meeting. Childress needed some help from the tire company for a driver he wished to put in his racecar. The driver was Dale Earnhardt. Childress had been running his own race team as the owner and driver, but he saw an opportunity to get out of the car and give Dale Earnhardt the wheel. Wrangler was already on board as the sponsor, but the team could not complete their deal unless Phil agreed to give them a budget for tires.

"So here I am, only in this job for two years and not able to really approve tire budgets. I asked if they could just wait awhile for the answer, but they were urgent in their request. They had to have the deal put together by the next day."

Phil frantically started thinking. He knew Dale Earnhardt had the talent to be a racing superstar. He felt he could not let his friend Richard down, and he felt the merger would bring success. But there was no budget left for the year, and he had no authority to make the decision.

"I was sitting in this hotel room racking my brain, and all of a sudden I came up with an idea. A.J. Foyt had just been involved in a terrible accident while at Michigan International Speedway. He cut his forearm badly and would need the remainder of the year to heal properly."

Foyt had a large tire budget allocated to him for life due to him bringing Goodyear into racing in the modern age. A.J. was golden to Goodyear, and he had a budget set aside for him whenever he wanted to race. Phil took a chance and started to compute the math in his head. They needed 14 tires for the amount of races they wanted to run.

"I said yes out loud, then I thought, 'What did I just say? I'm not supposed to be able to do this. I'm scared to death!'"

Richard yelled out, "That saves me; I can do this." Phil ventured out the hotel room door and entered his own room. He didn't sleep half the night. His boss would be at the race the next day and he needed to tell him what he had done. To make matters worse, the president of Goodyear was flying in. While eating lunch just before the race, Phil approached his boss, Leo Mehl.

"I said, 'Boss, I did something.' With great authority he yelled out, 'What?' and I explained what happened. He said, 'Good'. That's all he said."

Phil's heart was relieved and he felt good that he brought money to Childress and helped out Dale.

Yes, it was just a simple act on intuition that Earnhardt would become a superstar and an act to just help out a friend struggling to keep his race team alive, but Holmer realized something.

"Any time you help somebody, you can't hurt yourself. That's the way I look back on it now."

It's a simple life lesson that maybe we don't venture into often enough. A simple act of kindness could really help change someone's path in life. Phil later learned that one of those bodies sitting quietly in the dark in that hotel room meeting was Dale Earnhardt. They became good friends for many years, and Dale was a strong supporter of Goodyear tires throughout his amazing career. You can't hurt anything by just being nice.

17

RON
HORNADAY

"LIVING BY A MOTTO"

...

When you walk into NASCAR driver Ron Hornaday's office in North Carolina, a fluorescent sign shines Ron's motto for life: "Live Everyday Like It's Saturday." Hornaday didn't get into racing easily, and he lived a hard lifestyle in California trying to make a name for himself. But his outgoing and fun loving attitude kept him in the right people's minds and eventually got him a phone call from NASCAR's best.

"Every time I race, it's like a dream to me."

Hornaday had some racing roots. His father competed at the Late Model level in the Valencia, California, area where Hornaday grew up. He also met his wife, Lindy, at the track, where their fathers competed against each other.

"Lindy and I got married at a young age and had children pretty early. I had to quit racing two or three times in the beginning because I couldn't afford to keep shoes on my kids' feet. I couldn't get a better home for my family. I really have to give all the credit to Lindy; she kept doing whatever it took for us to go racing."

Lindy would work as a florist during the day and do nails at night to save additional money. Ron would tell his wife they couldn't go racing, but Lindy would all of a sudden come up with $5,000 for tires because she'd saved all of her earnings to help her husband. She also influenced Ron to quit fixing other people's racecars and bring his efforts home to build his own race machines. That got Ron focused on his personal career and encouraged him to get his name known. Ron and Lindy focused their efforts toward any televised races after NASCAR champion Darrell Waltrip gave Ron some advice in Phoenix.

"In 1994, I went to the Winston West race in Phoenix and ran into Darrell Waltrip to ask him how I could get noticed and find a ride out of North Carolina. He told me to try finding some races that were on television, do the best I could, and maybe get noticed."

Hornaday ran some more NASCAR Winston West events, NASCAR Featherlite Southwest Series races, and even visited a couple of the NASCAR SuperTruck Series (as it was called then) exhibition events. It wasn't until the Tucson Winter Heat series in December 1994 that Hornaday displayed his unbelievable talent. He basically dominated and took home the trophy in 12 of 13 races in the Late Model division. December was a time of year when all NASCAR divisions take a break, so all eyes in the racing world were on Ron Hornaday. Then a display of Ron's carefree attitude brought him another break.

"I saw Richard Childress at a track out west for a Legends Car celebrity race. He was going to have to run a really bad car, so I went and found him a decent piece to drive. Richard went on to win. He got a trophy and was pretty excited, so he said, 'Anything I can do for you, let me know.' I had seen Mike Skinner running a Truck in Tucson and told Childress he could help me. I heard Dale Earnhardt was starting a truck team, so I asked Richard Childress to have Dale call me."

Richard already had the answer for Ron. He told Hornaday to not worry, he'd already told Earnhardt about him! The next day, Dale Earnhardt called Hornaday's race shop. The only problem was that Ron's crew thought it was a prank.

"There was a guy that was an announcer at the Late Model track I ran. He would always call up my shop and pretend to be Richard Petty, and my employees would hang up every time he called. When Dale called, the guys thought it was another joke so they hung up on Earnhardt."

When Ron got to the race shop he asked if Dale Earnhardt had called. The guys all laughed until Hornaday yelled out, "No really, he's supposed to call me!" Around 1 pm that afternoon Earnhardt called back.

"Dale asked me what I was planning to do that week. I told him I had to get my racecar ready for the weekend, but Dale told me no. He told me to not worry about that car and fly on up to North Carolina."

Early the next morning, Ron got an overnight package with a letter from Dale Earnhardt Inc. and a first class airplane ticket to North Carolina. Hornaday had one problem: he'd never been on an airplane in his life, with the exception of a flight to Hawaii for his honeymoon. He was scared to death. The fear quickly wore off when he arrived in North Carolina and Dale Earnhardt himself picked Ron up. With his feet resting on the dashboard of his truck and dressed in a tuxedo, 'The Intimidator' was signing autographs when Hornaday walked up to enter the truck.

"Dale had all seven of his NASCAR Winston Cup championship trophies in the back of his truck. He had just shot a commercial for Goodyear. We took off down the road and I had no idea where I was. Earnhardt went flying down the road passing people and then this truck cut him off. The next thing I know, he runs into the back of the guy."

Ron was stunned and asked Dale, " Man, what are you doing?" Earnhardt looked at Ron and said, "That man is dating my daughter and I don't like him!"

Dale drove up to his 400-acre property and showed Hornaday where the race shops were to be built. He also showed him the location for the new truck team. Within minutes, Hornaday was offered a job to drive Earnhardt's Truck. A few minutes later he was signing a two-paragraph agreement to join the team.

"Getting that phone call from Dale and starting the truck series was a huge turning point in my life. Everyone in the series was really trying to make a name for themselves. It was like, when the green flag dropped, we raced every lap like it was the last lap."

Hornaday also learned that you can't stay mad at someone after a racing mishap.

"Mike Skinner and I would always go for the win. We'd come back after each race with two battered trucks, but we were still having a beer or soda pop after the race. I learned racing is like your family. You can't get mad. You know how you get mad at your kids and you spank them and put them to bed, but you still love them? You have to wake up the next morning and kiss them, make them breakfast and tell them what they did wrong. That's the way I look at racing."

Ron strongly feels that after the heat of the battle, you have to let it go. He knows that he has to see the same person the following week, not to mention 36 weekends out of the year.

"I don't care if it's before the race, I like to kid around with everybody. I like to have fun, and if you don't have fun, then you shouldn't be doing it."

I wouldn't say Ron Hornaday is a pushover with his carefree attitude. He's known as one of the most aggressive racers in all three top NASCAR racing series. He'll get you on a restart or place a rubbed tire mark on many racecars during an event. He also captured two NASCAR Craftsman Truck Series championships, in 1996 and 1998, so obviously his motto in life equals success. His outlook upon life made Ron many good friends, which led to many good contacts in his career. So maybe the next time someone makes you mad, you'll remember Ron Hornaday's motto and smile as you say, "Live everyday like it's Saturday." I know I will. I just may have to take a deep breath and grit my teeth first.

JIM
HUNTER

"THICK SKINNED"

. . .

I f you look up the term "thick-skinned" on Dictionary.com, it reads: 1. Having a thick skin or rind. 2. Not easily offended. 3. Largely unaffected by the needs and feelings of other people; insensitive. That is how I will now answer my friends when asked how we handle the racing business.

After a tumultuous year in my husband's racing career of pretty much no ups and many downs, I began to dwell upon one of our most asked questions: how do we do this? My husband's racing luck is about the same as Willie Coyote in the "Road Runner" cartoon. He just got fired from his NASCAR Winston Cup ride, yet I can still laugh daily about something. I had not sunk into a deep depression and my husband was still being kind and loving. In all reality, life was still good and I was determined to keep it that way.

Now, I am not saying I didn't have my moments, and one in particular led me to visit a good friend in the NASCAR corporate offices. I knew a few minutes spent with this veteran in the business would freshen up my outlook and attitude – and I figured he would have a good story for this book. So, first things first. What incident led me to realize I needed a little thicker skin?

While Mike was testing a NASCAR Winston Cup car for a small racing operation in Indianapolis, Indiana, I did get what I call a little redneck on a race fan. I decided to go to a supermarket for some groceries while Mike tested in the afternoon. We were traveling by motorcoach to Truck races and visiting race shops for any possible job opportunities in the racing world. Out of milk and lunchmeat, I entered the grocery store and caught a glimpse of a Kodak Racing stand-up poster of my husband. Even though I knew he no longer was the driver for that race team, I felt a sense of pride that my husband was still recognized as one of the NASCAR Winston Cup Series regulars. He was also rather handsome in this poster, and I grabbed my cart thinking, "That's my awfully cute hubby standing over there!"

Then I heard a lady approach the Kodak Film Processing counter. She yelled out to the clerk, "Don't you get any flack over that stand-up?" The clerk had no idea what the race fan was referring to. She again yelled out, "You should take that stand-up down because it's Mike Skinner and he just got fired!" I really don't know what came over me, but I felt the need to voice an opinion. I strolled over toward the woman and, as politely yet sternly as I could, told her that Mike Skinner was just fine standing over there and Kodak was a wonderful company and sponsor that would probably not be too upset to still have him as a representative. I rambled on a few other thoughts about my feelings regarding the situation, and before turning away, I told the lady that I knew all of these things because Mike Skinner was my husband!

Well, maybe that wasn't the most polite thing to do, but it did feel quite good, and I got a really hard laugh out of Mike that evening when I discussed my encounter over dinner. I didn't realize the need for a thick skin until I met with NASCAR's vice president of corporate communications, Jim Hunter. You may not know who Jim Hunter is, but if you follow the sport, I am sure you have heard from him. Jim has to handle all of the criticism and all of the hype that is thrown at NASCAR by the media and its fans daily.

If anyone in racing carries a thick skin, it's those who work behind the closed doors at NASCAR's headquarters in Daytona Beach, Florida. They don't get days off, they work relentless hours and they shape our sport into the entertainment we all thrive on every Sunday afternoon – and they get very little thanks for it.

I scheduled an interview with Jim one Friday afternoon for the book and to get some advice on my project, since he was also a published writer. The NASCAR Winston Cup Series regulars were qualifying in Watkins Glen that afternoon, and neither Mike nor I were in New York for the race. Mike was still in between rides, so we stayed home in Daytona Beach for one last weekend before a new opportunity as a temporary driver in the #01 Army Pontiac would be available at Michigan the following weekend. When I left Jim's office, I realized what being thick skinned is all about and why it can help all of us on a daily basis.

Jim Hunter has worked in racing for over 30 years. He started in South Carolina as a sportswriter for newspapers and continued on through the ranks as a public relations manager for Dodge and eventually in numerous jobs within NASCAR and its racetracks. Today, he is still guiding the sport as one of its key managers. He has no ego, and I've never heard him say a bad word about anyone. What he does have is thick skin. He will tell you he learned how to handle the business from his boss, Bill France Jr.

"Bill France Jr. had a great influence on me for his work ethic and sense of family. Most importantly, he learned early on that you have to have a passion for this business because it's so competitive. In a sense, it's so cutthroat, but by the same token, you have to spend your time working with and around the same people week in and week out, so you have to learn to let your raw emotions roll off your shoulder."

Jim experiences disgruntled drivers and invasive reporters daily. Sometimes, the same person that offered a smile one week is yelling at him the next. Handling yourself in a professional manner is a must, and sometimes, pure wit can help loosen a little tension.

"Bill always had an old saying, 'Let me win this one.' Every once in a while, I would come back with, 'I'd like to win one.' Bill would just grin. One afternoon, I was lobbying hard with Bill over a rules change. If Bill had made up his mind, he would always ask, 'Do you want to vote?' This particular day, he and I were the only two people in the room, so I replied yes to the vote; it would be a tie."

Bill came back with an unexpected twist for Jim. He told him there would be no tie and reached into his desk drawer. Holding a necktie in his hand, he told Jim, "I always keep an extra one here so I can always pull it out in situations like these." Jim never forgot that day, and it taught him yet another trait that he so admired in Bill France.

"Everyone has an ego, and Bill has managed his ego better than any person with as much power and responsibility than anybody I have ever known. He cuts right to the chase and asks about just the facts. If we as a company make a mistake, he will say we might have screwed that up, but it's over and done with, so let's move on."

In the modern era of today, that may come off as being insensitive, but NASCAR looks at it as having a thick skin and not taking things personally. With a chuckle, Jim said he realizes they are like the government, and no one likes the government unless they are getting a refund check. NASCAR is about the only sport where interpreting the rules is a key factor in the results, and almost every decision the officials make in the sport are questioned. I didn't realize the personal pain that the officials take on until Jim brought it to my attention.

"How does a driver's wife feel when she picks up a newspaper and reads her husband is a loser or jerk? The officials' wives and families are faced with that too. The driver and the official have to be smart enough to let unfair criticism roll off their shoulders. You listen and then let it go. Then you need to filter out what you can do to prevent the matter from happening in the future."

This lesson is one of the more difficult actions we must learn to do in our lives. It is hard to be able to sit and listen to someone who is being very emotional and saying things you know are not true. You can't take it personally, even though in the heat of the moment, people want to make it personal. In all reality, something happens every day where learning to carry a thick skin can help out. It's human nature to allow your emotions to explode and be heard. Learning to control those emotions is really doing something, and I guess that's what I learned after visiting Jim that afternoon.

I walked into that supermarket in a good mood. I just wanted to buy some milk, but I allowed something very silly to unleash my emotions. So I apologize to that lady I vented to in the Indiana supermarket and hope she reads this chapter. I will also have a little more respect for the NASCAR officials the next time they make a call that I feel is unfair. And hopefully, I will no longer lash out at a race fan who feels Mike Skinner is a no-driving fool. Now, I can't promise those things, but I will try. Would rolling my eyes make my skin thin? I hope not, because it sure makes me feel better.

ERNIE
IRVAN

"APPRECIATION"

• • •

Is there anything more important to a NASCAR driver than winning the Daytona 500? For Ernie Irvan there is. He won the "500" among many other NASCAR Winston Cup races. He also was named one of NASCAR's 50 Greatest Drivers. He had the NASCAR Winston Cup Series championship about wrapped up in 1994 until he suffered a near life-ending accident at Michigan International Speedway. Severe head injuries forced this NASCAR great to retire at an early age, but he will tell you today there is something far more important than winning America's greatest race.

"All of the Daytona 500 victories in a lifetime do not amount to what your kids can bring to you. I never realized how important family was until I made my life changing decision to walk away from the racecar."

I walked into Ernie Irvan's barn on July 9, 2003, with a little caution in my step. Would he be smiling? Will he want to talk about his days as a NASCAR Winston Cup driver? Will he be healthy? But what I walked into was a happy and content man - and a proud father. Ernie welcomed me with a smile on his face and quickly shared with me his two children's hobbies. Ten-year-old Jordan shows horses; five-year-old Jared just completed quarter-midget racing school. Both children showed me their prized possessions: beautiful show horses and a sleek quarter midget painted in flames. Ernie Irvan boasted in pleasure as he walked me around his property, letting his children show off their interests. After five minutes with the Irvans, I realized there is a life after racing. I also saw the importance of family.

Ernie Irvan was a take-no-prisoners kind of driver. He was aggressive on and off the racetrack, and he was winning. After replacing the late Davey Allison in the coveted Robert Yates Racing #28 Havoline racecar, Irvan was dominant in the 1994 NASCAR Winston Cup Series point standings. Then disaster struck. Irvan crashed hard into the wall at Michigan International Speedway during a practice session. Many in the garage area thought Ernie Irvan would never speak again, but he proved everyone wrong. He also proved the doctors wrong.

"I always thought bad wrecks happened to everyone else, so I would be fine. I ended up really hurt physically and with severe head injuries. The doctors told me that if I were ever able to drive my little girl to school then that would be a successful recovery."

Being a true competitor, Ernie told the doctors they did not understand. He would get back to racing. The doctor's again told Ernie that with his massive head injuries, the chances of him racing again were slim to none. They repeated to Ernie that he should focus on just being able to drive his little girl to school.

"I was devastated. There was no way I would be satisfied with that. I told the doctors I would drive again."

Ernie did just that. Within one year, Ernie Irvan returned to NASCAR racing.

He also beat the track that nearly took his life by winning at Michigan International Speedway in the same year of his comeback, proving the doctors wrong.

"It wasn't anything like I was a super human, being that I made the comeback. It was just because God allowed me to be able to race again."

Irvan continued to drive and enjoy the sounds of the screaming race fans. But in 1999, the same racetrack opened up its vicious jaws during a practice session, and once again, Ernie Irvan was pulled out of a crashed racecar and carried away on a stretcher. This accident was not as severe, but it did have Irvan considering his racing future. Ernie returned home to North Carolina after the accident and took his little girl to school.

"I had just dropped Jordan off at school, kissed her goodbye like I did each morning, and headed to the doctor's office with my trainer."

The same doctors told Ernie something different after this accident. They told him he proved them wrong the last time, so they would not tell him what he could or could not do. They ended up telling Ernie to do whatever he thought he needed to do, but Ernie noticed they were quiet and hesitant about giving him the freedom to make his decision. While Ernie was driving home, he made probably the most important decision of his life.

"I had never realized how important it was to drive Jordan to school until that morning. I felt the smartest thing I could do was to be alive for my children. I felt I needed to be a part of their lives. If I would have continued to go race and had another accident, I most likely wouldn't be here today."

While driving, Ernie called his wife, Kim, at home. He told her he had something to tell her, and as simple as it sounds, he told Kim he was going to retire. She didn't believe her husband and yelled out a "yeah, right!" and hung up the phone. She had wanted Ernie to retire long before this and felt he was just joking. One hour later, he walked into his home where Kim met him with the one question: "What did you say?" Ernie replied, "I said I am going to retire." Kim immediately embraced her husband and told him that was probably the smartest thing she'd ever heard. She also sealed his decision by telling him she'd be right beside him and support his decision. One week later, she did just that in

Darlington, South Carolina, when she sat next to her husband during a press conference to announce his retirement.

"I feel very fortunate to talk about what driving a racecar brought to me and what I did for racing. I got to make my own decision to retire, and everyday, I realize it was the smartest thing I did. Dale Earnhardt got me involved with Winston Cup racing. We usually took our daughters to school on the mornings we were in town. We would always just casually wave as we passed by one another. I didn't realize how important that was until Dale was gone. He can never take her to school again."

Ernie Irvan now has a career; his career is putting family first. He is involved with his children's lives. He knew the chances of him overcoming another serious head injury were poor, so he made a wise decision. He chose to enjoy life and appreciate his accomplishments.

"Being able to watch my kids grow up is more important than winning the Daytona 500."

Ernie admits that he never realized how much he enjoyed the race fans cheering every weekend when he entered his racecar until it was over, but he knows he was one of NASCAR's greats.

"Those wins are in the record books, they can't change that."

When I walked away from Ernie Irvan's barn where I recorded our interview, I looked back. Ernie went back to work. He took his son and daughter's hands and disappeared into their horse barn. Life is good for Ernie Irvan.

DALE
JARRETT

"FAITH"

. . .

NASCAR Winston Cup Series driver Dale Jarrett is a NASCAR champion. He has won the Daytona 500 twice and kissed the bricks in Indianapolis after winning the Brickyard 400. He has many victories on his stat sheet, but to him, victory is faith. How he rediscovered his faith is the story that Dale wished to share and hopefully pass on to other believers.

In 1991, Dale Jarrett was driving in the NASCAR Winston Cup Series for the Wood Brothers. Jarrett had replaced an injured Neil Bonnet and was thankful to be in such a position. For Dale, the Wood Brothers had helped to resurrect his career in NASCAR Winston Cup racing. The opportunity was one that Dale would never forget, but brighter things were in his future; he just didn't know it yet. In April of the same year, famed NFL coach Joe Gibbs visited a race in Talladega, Alabama. Being a fan of football and all sports in general, Jarrett got the opportunity to meet Gibbs just before the race.

"I just thought it was an opportunity to meet someone for a quick minute that I'd looked up to as a football coach. I figured that would be the last time I'd ever see or hear from Joe Gibbs."

Jarrett was wrong. Little did he know, Gibbs was looking to own a race team and he had his eye on Jarrett. In June, Dale Jarrett got a phone call.

"I'd had a bad day at the race in Dover, Delaware. My wife, Kelly, was already in bed asleep and the phone rang. The voice on the other end said, 'Can I speak to Dale?' I said, 'This is he.' And the voice responded with, 'This is Joe Gibbs.' I kind of laughed because I had many friends that played tricks and I figured they were trying to make my day worse."

The voice was Joe Gibbs and he told Jarrett of his interest in owning a race team. Jarrett was impressed that such a hero of his would consider him to drive, but felt an obligation to stay with the Wood Brothers since they had been so kind to him. Gibbs didn't give up and insisted that Dale just sit down and talk. Dale agreed.

"Joe Gibbs and three gentlemen from Interstate Batteries were in the meeting. He already had a sponsorship lined up and didn't even have a race team yet. When we were in the meeting, I expected them to ask me about my competitive spirit, my abilities as a driver or how well I could represent the sponsor. Those questions came up eventually, but the first question I got was, 'Are you a Christian?'"

Dale found the question to be a little odd in such an interview, and he hesitated in his answer.

"It would have been easy to go say, 'Yea sure,' but I felt the next question was

CHAPTER

21

JIMMIE
JOHNSON

"SET THE STAGI

• • •

Jimmie Johnson introduced hims
NASCAR Winston Cup Series
with a major upset. In Februar
the Rookie of the Year candidate took t
position for the Daytona 500. One of h
able life lessons paid off in one day and
attempt, but many well thought-out st
made his ultimate goal possible.

going to be something to back that up. I didn't want to back myself into a corner. I felt I needed to be up front and honest. I wanted to give the right answer, and the right answer was the truth."

Dale grew up in a Christian home, but he felt he could not sit and say he was following the Lord in the right way at that time. As the meeting concluded, Dale told Gibbs that he believed in God, but didn't know if he was practicing religion as he should. Gibbs appreciated his honesty. Dale went home and told his wife about the question he was asked in the meeting. It caused the two of them to think about their faith, and Jarrett started to feel that Gibbs' offer was more than just a chance to drive for another team. He ended up signing a contract with Gibbs, and by January 1992, Dale and his family were at the Superbowl. This was a perk that went along with driving for the famous Washington Redskins football coach, but there was more at this specific game.

"On Saturday night before the football game, the players had their chapel service. Coach Gibbs and a number of Washington Redskins players were present. Myself, Kelly, my sister Patty, and Patty's husband (and my crew chief) Jimmy Makar heard the most powerful speaker that night. Without knowing that the others did it, we were all asked to close our eyes and rededicate our lives to the Lord. All four of us stood up. Well ... that was what that first meeting was all about. It was a lot more than just getting an opportunity to drive for Joe Gibbs. It was an opportunity for me to get my life in order."

It was a life changing experience for Jarrett and his family. Dale and Kelly decided to bring their children up in the Christian home they had strayed from. At the same time, Dale had a good job and a lot of stability in his life.

"A lot of people get caught up in what they are trying to achieve and end up losing sight of things. Joe Gibbs helped me realize this and I began to look at things differently. I had faith."

Gibbs and Jarrett went on to see great success, including a Daytona 500 victory in only their second year as a team.

"So many times, we think we are in charge, but basically we are not. I thought I could make the right decisions and that I could get the job done without any help, but there never really was that peace of mind. It wasn't until I

started to realize that what helped me as a youngste
When I got back to that, I was able to accept the bad
a few more good days."

There is no doubt in Dale Jarrett's mind why Joe
and today he uses this story as a platform to help oth

"When I made the decision to join Gibbs and his n
tations. I felt, 'This guy's a football coach. I know he i
he understand racing?' I explained to him during on
in the NFL there are 14 winners every Sunday. In
winner each Sunday and 42 losers. Gibbs made me r
racing that way. Sometimes there are days when se
days, 10th feels victorious."

Gibbs' influence brought more peace to Jarrett's
was better for his family. He also learned that whe
you look for those little victories and have a little fai

(Top) A.J. Foyt poses with his NASCAR Winston Cup Series car in 1989. (Bottom) After retiring as a driver, Foyt was still driven to compete and formed his own race team, which currently field cars for A.J.'s grandson, Larry Foyt, pictured here on A.J.'s right.

Betty Jane France with her husband, NASCAR Chairman Bill France. Mrs. France remains active as NASCAR's assistant secretary at the sanctioning body's headquarters in Daytona Beach, Fla.

Bill France Jr. learned many lessons from his dad, NASCAR founder "Big Bill" France, before taking the reigns of the sanctioning body in 1972. Some lessons were large, and some were "nickel and dime" – but all were equally significant in molding the man who would guide NASCAR into the 21st century.

Crew chief Kevin Hamlin (left), Kevin Harvick and team owner Richard Childress (right) claim victory in Atlanta in 2001. It was Harvick's third NASCAR Winston Cup Series event.

NASCAR President Mike Helton has gained the respect of everyone in the NASCAR garage largely due to his under-standing that relationships are paramount in balancing the many facets associated with the sport.

You have to know Phil Holmer for the right set of Goodyear tires! A fixture in the sport for many years, Holmer believes in doing good things for others.

Once the engines fire, there's no doubt Ron Hornaday is a fierce competitor. But when the motors fall silent, Ron's endearing carefree attitude makes him one of the more popular drivers in the NASCAR garage. It also helped him land a ride driving for Dale Earnhardt!

Jim Hunter has been around stock car racing most of his adult life and, as the current vice president of corporate communications for NASCAR, he understands that, sometimes, you simply have to take things for what they are and just move on.

Ernie Irvan strolls the NASCAR garage with daughter Jordan.

Dale Jarrett shows off his 1993 Daytona 500-winning hardware with team owner Joe Gibbs.

(Top) Dale Jarrett (center) celebrates his first career NASCAR Winston Cup Series win at Michigan in 1991 with Wood Brothers principals (from left) Leonard, Len, Eddie and Glen Wood.
(Bottom) After two seasons with the Woods, Jarrett moved to Joe Gibbs' Interstate Chevrolet, a ride he kept for three years.

Jimmie Johnson and crew chief Chad Knaus (right) hoist the winner's trophy in the 2003 edition of NASCAR's all-star event, The Winston.

(Top) Jimmie Johnson and car owner/teammate Jeff Gordon contemplate chassis adjustments to the #48 Lowe's Chevrolet.
(Bottom) Kevin Harvick (left) and Jimmie Johnson offer mutual congratulations after the two young stars captured the front row for the 2002 Daytona 500, with Johnson on the pole in only his fourth NASCAR Winston Cup Series start.

(Top) The only thing that made Bobby Labonte happier than capturing the 2000 NASCAR Winston Cup Series title was sharing the joyous occasion with his son, Tyler.
(Below) In spite of his busy schedule as a NASCAR superstar, Bobby Labonte never sacrifices the chance to make his fans happy.

Randy LaJoie celebrates a NASCAR Busch Series victory at Daytona International Speedway.

It's not a wrong perception that Mark Martin is a fierce competitor.

RANDY
LAJOIE

"COMMITMENT"

...

In the sport of auto racing, success determines your value to a race team. Your relentless commitment to make it in the NASCAR Winston Cup Series determines your worth. Giving all of your time to accomplish this goal is a must. Commitment to the racecar and team means everything – unless you are Randy LaJoie. Don't take that last comment the wrong way. Randy LaJoie is a NASCAR champion. He is committed to his job, but his first commitment is to his family, and it's a decision most of us in the NASCAR garage admire.

In 1999 Randy LaJoie was a two-time NASCAR Busch Series champion and a threat to take the checkered flag each weekend he got behind the wheel. Not only could this stock car talent drive a racecar, he could also entertain fans with his quick wit and humorous outtakes in any interview. LaJoie was a crowd favorite. So why did he not have a NASCAR Winston Cup ride? Randy did attempt the premier racing series in 1995, but didn't find the chemistry needed with the team to run well. After 14 races, Randy was asked to leave the team.

"My first phone call was to my attorney, the second was to Busch Series car owner, Bill Baumgardner. Bill knew Johnny Benson was leaving his organization after winning a Busch championship. He guaranteed me a job for the next season."

The combination was victorious. In 1996 and 1997, LaJoie took the NASCAR Busch Series championships. Along with racing success, Randy received another gift: time with his family. With his wife, Lisa, of 14 years, he began spending Sundays with his two sons. Go-kart racing, swimming and going on an annual two-week motorcoach adventure across the country were the highlights in Randy's life.

1999 brought a season full of turmoil for LaJoie. Inadequate finishes and miscommunication started to plague the championship team. He knew he was ready for a change. Running the NASCAR Winston Cup circuit became an option again, but this time, LaJoie had a taste of commitment to his family. After a Sunday afternoon of attending church, riding go-karts and swimming with his two sons, Randy decided to take a rest on the couch to watch the NASCAR Winston Cup Series race. Randy's oldest son, Corey, was nine years old at the time and joined his father to check out the racing action on television. The television pit reporters began to cover a pit stop of a team with which LaJoie had an offer.

"I looked at my son and said, 'I could drive that car next season.' Corey responded that it was a good team and he was pretty excited about the opportunity, but wasn't excited about Dad giving up his time. He wasn't too enthused about the opportunity."

Then Corey turned into an agent. He looked at his father and began to ask questions.

"Well ... do we still get to go jump on the trampoline, race my go-kart and swim on Sundays?" Randy responded with, "No, that's out of the question; I will be working."

Then the second question: "What about our motorcoach tour during the summer?" Dad once again responded with another no. Corey then looked at LaJoie with apprehension and told him he would have to think about it. Next, Randy's youngest son, Casey, approached the decision bench.

"My six year old looked at me and said, 'Why would you want to do that?' I explained to him that I could make a whole lot of money. Casey reminded me I already had what I needed. He asked, 'Don't you already have a lot of money?' I told him yes and he came back with, 'then why do you need more?'"

Randy looked at his wife and said with a chuckle, "OK!" It took a six year old to make Randy realize he didn't need more.

"My banker at the time thought I was nuts. I had the opportunity to go Cup racing, but I chose my kids. Your kids grow up so fast. I've had more fun watching and playing with my kids on Sundays, and I could never put a price tag on that. Money wise, I sacrificed a lot, but to see my kids hit their first home run or go bowling and see them get a strike; I can't replace those moments."

Luckily, LaJoie's second opportunity was to get hooked up with the Kimberly-Clarke/Kleenex sponsorship at Evans Motorsports. The chance to run with another good NASCAR Busch Series organization made the decision even easier. In 2001, LaJoie won the NASCAR Busch Series race in Daytona, and on Sunday, he enjoyed an afternoon with his family.

"We don't extend ourselves now because we want more, when we've got plenty. We're very blessed with what we have and my kids mean more to me."

My husband, Mike, and I have looked at one another many weekends and joked that Randy LaJoie is the smartest one in the NASCAR garages. He found the happy medium to race his dream, make a good living at it and still be home every weekend. If only all of us could feel content with what we have and enjoy what your family can offer.

MARK
MARTIN

"PERCEPTIONS"

...

Mark Martin has had his share of success and heartache over his NASCAR Winston Cup career, but it took a day of excitement mixed with a sour ending to give this driver his first taste of the importance of perceptions.

In July 1981, Mark Martin was a dominant force in ASA racing and, along with his team, entered a NASCAR Winston Cup race in Nashville. The team had run two previous NASCAR Winston Cup events, one in North Wilkesboro plus the season's first Nashville race. The racecar was an altered version of his ASA car.

"We really didn't know what we were doing. We didn't have anyone from NASCAR helping us on the car, and we ended up sitting on the pole!"

With only two NASCAR Winston Cup events under his belt, Mark gleamed in excitement over his starting position. The only problem was the fact that Mark had no experience in what comes along with winning a pole. As he re-entered the garage to join his teammates, a van pulled up.

"These guys in a Busch Beer van came and whisked me away. I was down around the racecar because I was one of the mechanics. At that time, it was only myself and three others working on the cars. I jumped right in the van and didn't tell anyone where I was going because I had no idea what I was doing."

Mark was being introduced to the media. After a long press conference to explain who he was and where he came from, the van pulled up to take Mark back to the garage.

"I remember coming back in the tunnel of the Nashville Speedway, and as we reached the end of the tunnel, we met my guys. They were mad."

At that time in racing, the drivers and team members did everything together. They traveled, ate and even lived together. Mark and his crew would spend eight to 10 hours, seven days a week working on their racecar in a race shop that was behind their house. When the van carrying Mark reappeared through the track's tunnel, every other team had already packed up and gone back to their hotels. Mark's guys were furious because their driver had won the pole and then disappeared.

"I made a mistake by not knowing what I was getting into and got my guys mad at me for doing something we all could have only dreamed of. If you added up the limited facts they had, they felt I had deserted them and left them out of all the glory of our first Winston Cup pole. All I had really done was what I was asked to do by NASCAR."

Mark was devastated, and he quickly learned how the wrong perception of a situation can come with success. Later that evening, Mark went back to the hotel where he and his team were staying. His teammates were sitting by the pool and did not hesitate to give Mark the cold shoulder. It was a strange and uneasy evening for Mark, and it took some time to work out the sore feelings.

"They thought I was too good for them all of a sudden. I really worked hard on trying to explain to them what had happened. I basically got in that van and never even asked a NASCAR official what I was doing, where I was going, and when I would be back. I just didn't have the experience to know any better. That evening, I also realized that you have to watch perceptions because even if you don't change, people's perception of you can change quickly."

Since that day, Mark approaches similar situations in a thoughtful manner. His first consideration is never to allow self-importance to overshadow those who work toward his success. The other is to make your best effort to be honest and sincere, because you can't control other's perceptions of you.

"If someone doesn't admire or respect you for where you are in your life and career in the same manner that you respect them, then just shut it out. That day in the Winston Cup garage was my first taste of perceptions. It's always a hard thing to deal with, even in my career today. Nothing makes a person who is extremely successful feel better than for someone to say, 'That guy never changed after all of his success. He's still the same guy he used to be.' That just doesn't happen very often."

On Sunday morning, Mark and his team set their hard feelings aside and started their third NASCAR Winston Cup race. The tensions were resolved, but Mark was still crushed. His guys had a new perception of him as a driver, something he would have to handle for the rest of his career. I asked Mark if he remembered where they finished that race. He laughed at himself as he recalled finishing 11th.

"I felt that was a disgusting finish at that time. Then again, I didn't know what I was doing."

Martin quickly learned what he was doing two races later. He captured the pole position again, in Richmond, and this time he had a plan.

25

LARRY
McREYNOLDS

"SAY IT TODAY!"

...

In August 1994, Larry McReynolds felt like King Kong. Along with driver Ernie Irvan, Larry and the legendary #28 Havoline team felt almost invincible. They had already led more laps than any other NASCAR Winston Cup team in the garage, earned a couple of poles and won some races. They were starting the second half of the season and were battling back and forth with Dale Earnhardt for the championship. All of this success – just after a devastating tragedy. They had lost one of the most promising drivers in NASCAR history, Davey Allison, in a helicopter accident in 1993.

After the loss of Allison, the team had regrouped, reestablished their focus and fought hard to regain top status. Larry recalled even being disappointed when the 1993 season ended. Usually race teams are tired and ready for a break by the last race of the season, but the new combination of McReynolds and Irvan had success written all over it, and Larry was chomping at the bit to start the climb toward the 1994 title.

The "28" team had battled hard in only 13 months. Led by "Larry Mac," Ernie and the "28" bunch were in the hunt for the championship. Then, mid-season tragedy struck.

"We thought we were invincible – I never dreamt what would happen the next day."

It was early Saturday morning at Michigan International Speedway, and the weather was foggy and hazy. After posting one of their worst qualifying efforts of the year because the car was too loose in the corners, Larry set up the racecar purposely tight. He was a meticulous crew chief and knew that setting up the car in this manner would not only give his driver more confidence, but also give Larry more confidence for a thorough practice. The session began, and as Larry predicted, the car was too tight. They completed 10 laps, and Larry immediately got on the radio to instruct Ernie to bring it in. The driver did not respond.

"Ernie and I had this deal where whether we were going to run 10 laps or 15 laps, he would go and run through the next set of corners hard, and I could tell as he drove off into one that was what he was going to do."

With the early morning haze blinding Larry's view, his driver and best friend entered turn one.

"After I saw Ernie go into turn one, I remember looking at the red flag waving on the frontstretch. Raymond Fox, my car chief at the time, starting waving his arms. I looked at him like 'yea! I know there is a caution.' But he starting screaming, 'It's us, it's us!' That's when I got back on the radio and asked Ernie if he was ok."

According to Larry, a crew chief's worst nightmare is when the driver does not respond. Silence. That's when you try to think positive. It's not unusual for a driver's radio to become unhooked in an accident. Larry attempted to speak to Ernie three more times. As Larry began to walk off their trailer, he caught a glimpse of NASCAR official Buster Auton running out of the NASCAR trailer like a madman headed to the pace car. Team owner Robert Yates and Larry followed. As they drove wide open around MIS to get to the scene of the accident, Larry didn't think the car looked too bad.

"Steve Peterson, another NASCAR official, walked up to us and said to not go any further. It was like the sickest feeling in the world. I guess for a brief moment the selfish part of me was thinking about myself. This can't be happening to me again. I mean, damn, 13 months ago Davey was killed in a helicopter crash."

Then Larry started thinking about all the other people it was affecting.

"I started thinking about the race team. I started thinking about Ernie's wife, Kim, and their little girl, Jordan. I immediately walked over to the outside wall and threw my guts up."

The devastated team leader could not understand why this would happen twice in 13 months. Auton grimly gathered Larry and Robert back into the pace car. When they arrived back at the garage, they were told Irvan would be airlifted to Ann Arbor.

One thing is certain about the "NASCAR family:" You may fight on the racetrack and squabble in the pits, but when one of the family gets hurt, everyone hurts. Don Hawk, who was at that time Dale Earnhardt's business manager, approached Larry and Robert to see if there was anything he could do to help. The very opponent that was fighting Ernie for the championship came with a concerned heart. Don gathered Larry, Robert Yates, Ernie's wife and father, and the racing chaplain to hurry to the hospital.

"I remember riding to that hospital, and that hour and 20 minutes felt like about four hours. Nobody said a word in that car. I sat in the back seat on the driver's side and looked out the window, and all of a sudden, all my thoughts about the whole episode changed. They totally went away from racing; they totally went away from our race team and winning races."

In the extreme silence, Larry started to realize that he didn't care if Ernie ever did drive that racecar again. He just wanted to be able to talk to him again.

"I just wanted him to be able to be a friend to me, a husband to Kim, a father to Jordan, be a son to his parents. That's all that's important. If he can come back and drive a racecar, then that's the added bonus."

Ernie and Larry had become best friends, and Larry started to realize he had never told Ernie how much he appreciated all he had done for his race team. Ernie came in when the "28" crew was at rock bottom. This talented driver had given Larry's career new life. It was in the car when Larry realized a lesson that he carries dear to his heart and remembers in his everyday life.

"No matter how mad you are at a friend or loved one, whether it be a spouse or a child, your mom or your dad, don't leave your house or go away without letting them know that you care for them and love them. More importantly, if there is something that you want to tell someone, if there is something you're feeling or somebody you want to call, whether it's a friend or family member, don't put it off. You just may never get that chance again. Pick up the phone and call someone. You don't have to carry on a 45-minute conversation. Just tell them, 'Hey! I was thinking about you.'"

It was that very day in 1994 that Larry McReynolds observed this life lesson: Don't put off until tomorrow what you can do today.

"The last thing I ever dreamed was for Ernie Irvan to back out of that garage, go make a 10-lap run and never come back."

I guess I can relate to Larry on that situation. You put your driver, and in my case a husband, in a racecar before an event knowing anything can happen. You can't predict what life will hand you. Show your love and appreciation today. If you feel it, say it today.

Later that dark Saturday evening, a doctor gathered everyone in a small room and told Ernie's loved ones that there was a 10-to-15 percent chance that he would live. For three weeks, Larry spoke daily to Ernie's wife, Kim. While Ernie fought to recover, the medical team transported the weakened driver back to a Charlotte area hospital.

"One of the greatest moments in the world was about two and a half weeks after that. The phone rang and it was Kim. My first feeling was to just cringe, but she said to hold on, there was someone wanting to talk to me. It was Ernie, and you better believe I told him everything I wanted to let him know that very minute!"

MARTHA
NEMECHEK

"MOTHERLY ADVICE"

...

O n any given weekend, you can find
Martha Nemechek waxing the racecar
that her son, Joe Nemechek, drives. She
attends nearly every race adorned in a racing
shirt that displays her son's sponsor, car number
and colors. Martha is the ultimate racing mom.
I wanted to find out why she puts so much effort
into her family and how she views her dedication
toward her son's racing career. The first thought
that came to my mind was motherly love.

Joe and Martha Nemechek had four children: Joe Jr., Mark, John and one daughter, Marty. Born and raised in Florida, the Nemechek children were taught that the little things in life are the most important.

"My parents always taught me to focus on the little things and to always help people who were less fortunate."

Martha and Joe didn't have a lot when they first started their family. Joe worked two jobs and Martha worked as a bookkeeper and even took on some ironing to make additional money. She felt she needed to keep her children busy in activities to distract them from bad behavior. The boys chose motorcycle racing.

"When Joe was 13, he started motorcycle racing. Mark was 12 and John also started racing at the age of 12. Even our daughter, Marty, had a boyfriend that liked to race. We all did it together."

By the time Joe was 15, he started racing mini-stocks. His younger brother, John, admired his older sibling and told his mother that he, too, wanted to race stock cars. Mark chose not to race after an accident injured his legs in an earlier motorcycle race.

Martha and Joe started their own business about the same time. Even though the new business was a struggle in the beginning, Martha remained close to her son's racing ventures. Cooking for the team and just taking lots of pictures of their races became a mission from which Martha would not stray.

"There are many ups and downs in racing. Even though we didn't finish every race, or got wrecked, I would always go back to the shop with Joe and John. I was always in the shop helping to display family love."

She never realized how happy she would be that she spent the time and took all those pictures until she lost a child. Martha's son, John, lost his life tragically in a NASCAR Craftsman Truck Series race in 1997. His older brother, Joe, was already known as a famous NASCAR driver; John was on his way to join his brother in the NASCAR Winston Cup ranks.

"John had always told me, 'Momma, there are things I want to do with my life. One is be famous like Joe.' John always wanted to race right along with Joe. He wanted to be like the Wallace brothers. He also said he wanted to donate his organs if anything ever happened to him in a racecar. At that time, I told him I didn't want to talk about such things, but he insisted, telling me what he wanted to do."

Martha fulfilled John's wishes as she pleaded with her eldest son, Joe, to retire from the sport.

"I always told my children I wanted them to be happy in what they did with their lives. Of course, when John passed, I asked Joe to quit. He said, 'Mom, you can't ask me to; you always told me I had to be happy in what I did. Racing is in my blood. You were always there to help me. I would be happy if you and Dad were at my races to support me."

Martha had to accept whatever Joe decided on. Since he wanted to continue racing, she continued to go to the races, and she continued to wax Joe's NASCAR Winston Cup car before every race.

"Support is what your children need most, even if you may not think that's the right way or right decision. Just be there. I had to accept whatever they did in life. I wanted them to be happy. I always said, 'If you're happy, then I'm happy.'"

Knowing she had to continue following Joe on the race circuit, Martha still had to cope with the loss of her son, John.

"I was at the highest point in my life before I lost John. I had taken time away from our business to just travel and follow my children racing all around the country. When you lose someone, you go to the bottom, but you learn to cope. He's been gone six years now, and today, I try to help other people in need of support. I feel in my heart it's rewarding for me and it helps me cope with my own life."

Martha has 21 people she calls weekly or twice per month who have experienced a loss such as hers.

"When John died, I had a man call me from Oregon. He was a NASCAR official and had lost a daughter in an airplane crash. When he called, I thought, 'Oh dear, that's just another person that wants to know my business.'"

The man continued making his phone calls to Martha and sent letters of encouragement. He offered his time when Martha was struggling. It was a little gesture that helped her through such a hard time.

"That's why I call the people on my list today. I tell them I can be there to listen or just tell them what I went through."

Today, Martha and her husband, Joe Sr., continue to follow Joe in the NASCAR Winston Cup Series in their motorcoach. Nearly every weekend, I see Martha walking with the race team as they push Joe's waxed racing machine. She always smiles. The Nemecheks do take some weekends off to spend with their other children and grandchildren. Balancing her time can be hectic with our 38-week race schedule. There is no telling how many races this mom has taken in, but there is one race at which she hopes to be present.

"I have not been at the track for any of Joe's Winston Cup wins, but Joe has managed to give me a little support when he celebrates in victory lane."

If Martha isn't present, Joe's wife, Andrea, hands Joe a cell phone as soon as he gets out of his car.

"He always calls me and will say, 'Mom, I won!'"

Martha Nemechek feels she's accomplished a lot in her life because not many people can give the support she extends toward her children. Her motherly advice? Just make the little things important.

In her eyes, the Nemecheks are still together, and that makes her the luckiest mom in the world.

BENNY
PARSONS

"OBSESSION"

. . .

S imply just being in the right place at the right time can place you in a victorious circumstance, but what you do with that chance will determine your fate. 1973 NASCAR Winston Cup Series Champion Benny Parsons can prove such a life lesson. In one day his life changed drastically, all because some racers decided to stop by his father's gas station for a quick restroom break.

Growing up in North Carolina near the North Wilkesboro Speedway, Benny was aware of NASCAR racing. His father was a fan and, in 1948, took his son to see a stock car race. The experience was exciting for "BP" but not enough to trigger a desire to get involved with the sport. As Benny matured, he found himself without guidance on what to do with his life. He attended a short stint in college but found himself not willing to focus enough on his studies. With his parents living in Detroit, Benny packed up from his grandmother's home in North Carolina and moved north to Motor City.

"In 1960, I moved to Detroit with no guidance on what to do with my life. I got a job at one of the auto factories."

One Saturday morning, Benny found himself hanging out at his father's gas station. Two men, Wayne Bennett and Dick Gold, pulled up with a truck and a racecar on the back. They were only stopping to use the restroom.

"A 1960 Ford stock car! I was 19 years old and my eyes really lit up. Wow! Look at that – a race car!"

The sparkle in Benny's eyes must have caught the racers' attentions, for after Benny asked where they were racing, the two men, very innocent like, asked him the question that would change his life: "Do you wanna go?" Without even knowing Bennett or Gold, Benny ran home, grabbed a toothbrush and a change of clothes and jumped in the truck to head to Sun Valley Speedway in Anderson, Indiana.

"I got a full weekend introduction to stock car racing. We raced Sun Valley on Saturday night, then drove immediately to Dayton, Ohio, to race Sunday after-noon. I've often wondered what life would have been like if I hadn't been at that gas station that Saturday morning."

Benny continued to go with the two men and, after a while, became part of their race group.

"They saw I was excited to see a racecar. When you see that in a person, you want to fulfill their excitement."

Going from just hanging out to rolling tires and then graduating to working on their racecar, Benny Parsons became focused on stock car racing. The need to drive was just around the corner, and an obsession slowly started to develop.

Finally, one January morning in 1963, Dick Gold approached BP with an offer to drive. Gold had just bought a car from an old boy who was moving up in the ranks. He had a figure-eight quarter-mile racecar he needed to sell quickly in order to build a half-mile machine.

"I asked him how much he paid for this car. He responded, 'Fifty bucks, and it's only three blocks away.'"

The two drove toward a wooden garage where the vehicle was stored. It was an overcast morning, and Benny remembers his first thought about his first racing machine.

"The garage was dark, no artificial light to see inside. My first thought was, 'You were cheated.' The car was awful. The sides were beat off and the sheet metal all torn to pieces."

In the same year, Gold and Bennett invited Parsons to attend the Daytona 500. You could almost say this trip south capped off the desire to be more than a hired hand. Just being a spectator wasn't enough for this future champion.

"I was in the infield, hanging on the fence wanting to be on the other side so bad I couldn't stand it."

The enthusiasm came to a boil and Benny had a goal. He would run the Daytona 500. May 1963 brought his first race. It was a quarter-mile dirt track. Though his day ended on the first lap after spinning and jamming a gear, which led to a broken transmission, BP knew he had found an obsession.

"My mind was focused on the job at hand. When I raced that car in 1963, I found out what focus was all about, because all I ever wanted to do from that day on was run the next lap. If you have enthusiasm for something and then you become involved in it, you either get turned against it or you get obsessed. I became obsessed."

Obsession is the key to success?

28

MIKE
SKINNER

"HURDLES"

...

On the evening after being released from the #4 Morgan McClure Motorsports NASCAR Winston Cup car, I sat down with my husband, Mike, to gather his "Turning Points" story. We were fresh out of our airplane, leaving our vacation in the Sonoma Valley many days early. We had planned to get to the Sonoma, California, race five days early in order to enjoy a mid-season vacation, but Monday morning Mike was released from his race team. We immediately packed our bags and came home to begin the search for a new ride.

The ride home was somber and quiet. When we arrived home, or what we call paradise, Mike told me to get my tape recorder; he was ready to speak. I was happy to get the interview done since my book deadline was quickly approaching, and I knew he needed to vent after miserable 2002 and 2003 seasons. As soon as I pressed "play" on the recorder, Mike began his story with a life lesson that we all face daily.

"In life you face a lot of hurdles. Every time you jump over a hurdle you take a few steps and there's another hurdle. Sometimes they're taller and sometimes they're shorter, but they are always there."

In 1995, Mike Skinner was the driver to watch. He was leading the points and winning regularly in the inaugural season of the NASCAR Craftsman Truck Series and labeled an overnight success. Mike laughs at that label and explains his notoriety as a "twenty-year success." It wasn't overnight! Mike was 38 years old when he signed his first NASCAR contract with car owner Richard Childress, but he had been racing since his was 18. Born and raised in California, Skinner had aspirations of being a professional pool and billiards player. It was by accident and a car wreck on a side street in Susanville, California, that Mike caught the racing bug. A friend convinced Mike to buy back the wrecked 1971 Road Runner from the insurance company and turn it into a racecar for the local fairgrounds dirt track.

"I found I was a better racecar driver than pool player – at least I thought I was because I was superior over the competition at that time."

Becoming a professional racecar driver really wasn't in Skinner's thoughts. Mike was a well driller with his own business while winning races on the weekend. The winnings turned into some track championships, and Mike began to wonder if he could play with the boys in the NASCAR Winston Cup Series. The economy in Susanville was very bad, and a friend of Mike's, Terry Elledge, decided to put his race talents to better use and moved to North Carolina to build race engines. He encouraged Mike to do the same. By 1983, Mike packed his bags to move east and pursue his newfound dream to drive in the NASCAR Winston Cup Series, and it wasn't without the inspiration of his then wife, Beth.

"Beth told me to either become a racecar driver or quit complaining about it.

She told me, 'If you've got the guts to pursue this dream, then you're going to have to move to North Carolina where the real racing is.'"

Two weeks later, Mike and Beth headed east, but it was one of the first hurdles for Mike to cross over.

"I loved Susanville; the mountains and the country were beautiful. I had moved one other time, to Colorado, and when I came back I said I'd never leave, and here I was leaving again. It was hard for me to make that move even more because I also had a son (from a previous relationship) I had to leave behind."

Skinner got a job in the engine department at the Petty shop. He made $205 per week take-home pay – a far cry from the money he made with his well-drilling business. While building engines during the week, Mike would race a few Late Model events on weekends, but it wasn't NASCAR Winston Cup and started to wear on his dream. He could get numerous jobs with race teams, but it was as a body man or a tire changer, not as the driver.

"In 1984, I got a job on Rusty Wallace's Winston Cup team as a body man and tire changer. It was Rusty's rookie year, and it was a pretty big hurdle for me when I chose to leave that team because I like Rusty and knew Rusty would be a great driver. Darrell Bryant was the crew chief when I went in to give my notice. He told me I was a good employee and asked what it would take for me to stay with the team. I looked at him and told him Rusty's job was the only thing that could keep me. I moved to North Carolina to be a driver, not make Rusty Wallace popular."

Mike left the team and again started his own business with an old friend from California. This time he started a body shop. While winning various Late Model Stock Car races around the Carolinas, Skinner did make a few races in the NASCAR Winston Cup Series as his own car owner or with partnerships with friends. His first attempt was at Martinsville, Virginia, in 1986.

"Maurice and Richard Petty gave us some spare parts for our car. Even Richard Childress gave us some used tires off Dale Earnhardt's #3 car. It was a pretty big effort for us. We pulled into the garage with a dually pickup truck and stole milk crates from behind a supermarket to store all our spare parts. I think we were the only guys there in a pickup truck; everyone else had 18-wheelers by then. But we weren't embarrassed; we made the show and had a car capable of finishing in the top 10."

The spare parts turned tragic for Mike; he burned the gear during the race. He was upset but knew they made a good effort for their first NASCAR Winston Cup race.

Throughout the late 1980s and into the early 1990s, Mike continued to run various NASCAR events. His NASCAR Winston Cup efforts nearly sent him into bankruptcy, so he focused on running Late Model Stock events and a few NASCAR Busch Series entries for numerous car owners. Gene Petty, a cousin to the great driver Richard Petty, was one of the first car owners to notice Mike's tenacity and great talent. Gene owned one of the more prestigious Late Model racing operations in North Carolina and fielded one of the best drivers in competition. Mike saw an opportunity to catch Gene's eye.

"Gene Petty always had the best car and driver in Late Model. There was one race when I had to compete against his driver. They were three-tenths faster than anyone on the track, and I was looking at a third-place finish this particular race. A caution came out late in the race, and I said to myself, 'Now's my chance. I've got to get on the wheel and beat this guy.' Somehow or the other, with five laps to go, I found the power to win that race."

One week later, Gene Petty was sitting in Mike's front yard on a picnic table, waiting for Mike to come home from work and offer him a full-time ride in Late Model Stock competition. Mike accepted, and in the first race that Mike sat in Petty's car, he won. They won a track championship, in 1993, at Caraway Speedway in North Carolina. He finally had a full-time ride as a driver.

"Along the way, I jumped over a bunch of hurdles to get noticed. It would have been real easy to cave in and allow the rejections to devastate me and go back to California to drill wells. It's a lot harder to say, 'I'm going to make it. I'm going to keep going until I make this dream happen.'"

About the time Skinner felt the reality of his dream coming alive, the worst hurdle in his life took place. Halfway through 1994, Mike's mother, Frankie, called to report bad news.

"My mom called to tell me she had been diagnosed with cancer. She told me they were going to do an exploratory surgery and to not worry. I wanted to come home and stay with her, but she insisted that I run the next week's race in Myrtle Beach."

Frankie was not only Mike's mother, but his best friend too. She, more than anyone in his career, helped him pursue his dream to drive in NASCAR Winston Cup Series competition. When Mike needed money for tires, his mother would find the resources to make it happen. Taking orders from his mother, Mike planned to win the race in Myrtle Beach and fly home to California directly after to drive his mother home after her surgery.

"I went on and won that race. I found out later that about the time I took the checkered flag, my mom had passed on. She hung around until I won that race, then she gave up. I was devastated. I wanted my mom to see me make it as a driver. It seemed like every time I turned around, there was another hurdle to cross, but every time I knocked one over, I'd get back up and go on to the next one. I refused to give up. I would dig even harder to cross the next hurdle because I kept managing to always clear them."

As soon as Mike cleared the hurdle of his mother's sudden death, he got noticed by one of the sport's most noted car owners. The only problem was, he got the owner's intentions a little mixed up. While working for Gene Petty, Mike attempted a NASCAR Busch Series event in Charlotte. His attempt put him on the pole for the event, leaving newspaper headlines to read 'Mike Who?' For the first time, the NASCAR world started to take notice of Mike Skinner. Car owner Richard Childress saw the aggressive and rugged characteristics of Skinner and plotted to hire him for his NASCAR Craftsman Truck Series entry in 1995. Mike had no idea that NASCAR was developing a new racing series, so when Richard told him he wanted Mike to drive his truck, he blew it off. A few weeks later Richard called Mike.

"Richard asked me if I would be interested in driving his truck. Well, hell, I was stupid and figured he was talking about the truck that pulled Earnhardt's race car, so I said, 'I really appreciate your offer, but I am driving a Busch car right now and I don't want to drive no damn truck. If Earnhardt calls in sick or anything and you need somebody to drive that car, then give me a ring!'"

Again, a few weeks passed and a few frustrating NASCAR Busch Series races later, Mike started to realize just who had called him. He also learned about the new truck series that NASCAR was creating. Mike picked up the phone and called Richard Childress. With a chuckle he asked Richard if he'd found that truck driver yet. An interview was arranged and Mike's career would change forever.

"After an overwhelming tour of Richard's facility, he sat down and offered me the job. The offer blew my mind. I've never been a great poker player, but I sat straight-faced that afternoon and never changed my expression when he told me the money he could give me. In reality, I about fell out of my chair! I didn't want him to know that I was impressed, but the whole time I wanted to reach over and kiss him."

Mike Skinner had made another jump over a life hurdle. This jump was closer to his NASCAR Winston Cup dream than any other. Mike became an instant racing celebrity, winning more truck races and capturing more poles than any other driver in the series. They won the truck series' first national championship. It wouldn't be long before the NASCAR Winston Cup Series offers would come rolling in. In 1996, the opportunity arose, and Richard Childress Racing announced that Mike Skinner would run for Raybestos Rookie of the Year in 1997 with Lowe's Home Improvement Warehouse as his sponsor. They would be team #31.

In his first NASCAR Winston Cup Series event with the #31, Mike captured the Daytona 500 pole position and went on to clinch the Raybestos Rookie of the Year award. The future looked promising. The team captured more poles and many good finishes, but no wins that counted. They won in Japan two years in a row and they won qualifying races – just not a points event. Plagued with bad luck and some horrific crashes, Skinner was looking at a hurdle that seemed too high. Mike reached a peak when Larry McReynolds came to be the crew chief for the #31 bunch. They finished in the top 10 of the NASCAR Winston Cup Series standings in 1999 and 12th the year after, but Larry chose to take a career in broadcasting, and the team communication crumbled when Larry left.

"I was not 100 percent at the end of that year, Larry was not 100 percent at the end of the year, and in reality, I was really hurt physically and mentally. Richard replaced Larry. We never gelled, and we didn't have success. It was a big hurdle and ended up costing me my job."

Mike struggled and found himself looking for a new adventure in 2001.

"It was really tough to say goodbye to Richard Childress Racing. After the truck championship and success we did have, I felt like I would spend the rest of my racing years at RCR in some capacity or another. It was home."

Mike and RCR parted ways midseason. Mike had just suffered a severe injury to his knee and ankle at Chicago in early July, and Richard was kind enough to let Skinner stop racing and have surgery to repair his ailments in order to be strong for the 2002 racing season. Mike had the surgery, and while he recovered he looked for a new job. As a family, Mike and I were pretty quick to take the first opportunity that arose, the #4 Morgan McClure Motorsports seat. The United States had just been devastated by the September 11 terrorist attacks, and the economy was in jeopardy. We felt Morgan McClure had a strong sponsor in Kodak and agreed to sign a two-year contract with an option for a third year.

"I knew the '4' car would be a struggle. They had been a good organization in the early 1990s, but all of a sudden the multi-car teams figured out success with teammates. The team had not been competitive for a couple years. I took the job hoping I could make a difference."

Mike did tell car owner Larry McClure that he had no magic wand; he knew the problems were not in the driver. In fact, the drivers that had left the operation had gone on to other teams and won races. As a wife, it hurt to see Mike face such adversity. I would encourage Mike by telling him he was a NASCAR champion, and Mike would face the adversity from the media, his team, even his friends and keep a positive attitude.

"We had a rough time. I mean rough! I felt like we were so far behind. At Christmas time in 2002, Larry hired Tony Furr to manage the race team. I remember thinking it was the best gift I could receive. I really felt like Tony's addition would be pretty big."

Mike's feeling was right. Tony started to improve the whole team, and they kicked off Daytona testing in January 2003 as the fastest car on the track.

When the season started, the Skinner bad luck followed, and whenever the "4" car would have a good run, a wreck would take them out. Tony ended up leaving after the Bristol race in March. Newspapers reported he missed living in the Charlotte area, since Morgan McClure was based in Abington, Virginia, but Mike knew the real reason. He was not given the reigns to properly run the team.

"When Tony left, it took a lot of wind out of my sails, and I began to feel I was unable to communicate with the team."

We knew the next hurdle in Mike's career would be finding a new job. We didn't know the timing would come so soon in the year. We also knew it would be difficult. It would be a tough battle to get another competitive ride in NASCAR Winston Cup. On August 13th, doomsday for Mike Skinner became present. The race team took an untested car to Michigan. The team had no provisionals to make the race, so the group would have to make the field on time alone.

During practice they were borderline on the speed chart. As a team they made one last adjustment and, at the end of the day, failed to make the 43-car field.

"It was only the second time in my career on a full-time ride that I didn't make a race. I was pretty devastated."

In an effort to raise Mike's spirits, we flew to Susanville where it all began. We went to the beautiful mountains and played pool with some old buddies. Reporters called Mike all weekend to get his take on why they missed the race. I remember when the race started on Sunday afternoon. We were sitting in our hotel room in Reno, Nevada, packing to leave for Sonoma. I didn't think Mike would want to watch the event on television, but he turned it right on. He watched every lap like he was in the race, then he picked up the phone and called Larry. He explained to Larry that the media wanted stories, but he refused to badmouth the organization and we would carry on toward Sonoma to make the next race and get over the devastation of Michigan. Nothing else was really said, and we went onto Sonoma for the next race on the circuit. As soon as Mike took his first drink of coffee Monday morning, Larry called to simply say they were making a driver change. I heard Mike say that that was cool and hung up the phone. He sat on the hotel bed and with despair in his eyes said, "I just got fired; let's go home."

So over another hurdle Mike Skinner goes. My interview was about over, but Mike had to leave my tape recorder with one last statement.

"At this point in my life, I'm back in that spot where it could be real easy to hang my helmet up and say I've done OK, but I'm too damn stubborn and hard-headed. I'm not going to do that. I'm going to pursue the next opportunity and climb that next hurdle. I'm going to clear it and start the next chapter in my life. In all reality, it just gets back to, life's nothing but a bunch of hurdles. So far, I've knocked a few down. So far, I've jumped over many. My next goal is to climb over a new one."

We all face hurdles. This chapter is just a testament of a minute amount of the many jumps Mike Skinner had to clear to become a NASCAR Winston Cup Series driver. What is Mike's next hurdle? Who knows, but I can say that Mike Skinner has some unfinished business in racing: a NASCAR Winston Cup points win. So stay tuned, because you can bet that will be another hurdle he plans to clear.

JIMMY
SPENCER

"CAN'T WE ALL JUST GET ALONG?"

. . .

NASCAR Winston Cup Series driver Jimmy Spencer, better known as "Mr. Excitement," has had his fair share of on-track scuffles with fellow competitors. He earned his famous nickname for his aggressive style of driving and ability to never hold back a comment, positive or negative. He has spent many years on the NASCAR circuit and, though he may get a little picked on for being outspoken, he has learned a thing or two about people. Jimmy has always been honest. If you ask him a question, you will get a quick – and truthful – answer from this racer. It may make you mad or hurt your feelings, but Jimmy Spencer will tell you straight up how he feels about any given situation. I found his advice for this book to be simple and truthful: Learn how to get along with people to be successful.

"When I first started racing, I built and drove all my own cars. The further along I got into my career, the more successful I became. I began to win a lot of races. I didn't want to admit it then, but I got pretty set in my own ways. When you get into the higher levels of racing and you have to go to work for someone else, you start to realize it's not going to be done your way."

Arguments and disagreements can take a top racing team to the bottom in a matter of one week. In Jimmy's case, not getting along with the boss or his team members hurt his career for a long time.

"I used to get really mad at people and get into arguments because we weren't running good. Things were not getting done the way I felt they should."

A few years and a few race teams later, Jimmy started to realize that he was the driver and his primary focus was to just drive the car. It can be the same in any business situation. Once you realize that you are not the boss and your way is not always the right way, success could be right around the corner.

"Being outspoken has gotten me in a lot of trouble. I've learned to try to be quiet. There's so many times in a day where I want to say, 'I think my way is better,' but I just say it to myself."

I kept trying to get Jimmy to give me a specific story about the day he finally learned that getting along could make his career better, but he just kept telling me to make a story out of his comments. I thought about this for a while, and it finally hit me. During the 2003 Winston Open race, my husband, Mike, and Jimmy had two of the best cars on the racetrack. Both Mike and Jimmy are known as being rough and stubborn on the track, so when the two of them battled it out for position during the race, I held my breath. A little slide up the racetrack and a couple bangs later, Mike had nearly wrecked Jimmy.

The crowd was screaming with excitement as I stood wondering if "Mr. Excitement" would come back and wreck my husband in retaliation. The race ended a few laps later and neither Mike nor Jimmy won the race – and neither Mike nor Jimmy beat on one another's racecars during the cool-down laps.

I began to walk back to the team hauler to meet Mike as he pulled into the garage. On my way in, I passed Kevin Harvick. He was walking toward his racecar for The Winston all-star race. Since Mike did not win the Winston

Open, we were out of the running, so I ran up to Kevin and said, "Good luck. I guess I'll have to root for you to win now." With his ornery smirk, Kevin replied that I should probably run to the garage because Mike and Jimmy were in a brawl! Now, I know Kevin likes to pull a good prank on his friends, so I laughed at first and blew his warning off, but Kevin kept a serious look and insisted that he was not joking this time.

I took off running toward Jimmy Spencer. I don't know what I thought I could do if the two men were fighting. I guess I felt I needed to be the support for my racecar-driving husband. Out of breath and trying to keep my stiletto heels intact, I saw Jimmy calmly performing a television interview. I quickly looked around to make sure no one else saw my desperate attempt to see the big fight. I was embarrassed, but laughed at myself and the fact that I knew Kevin was laughing all the way to his car.

I caught Mike out of the corner of my eye and he, too, was performing an interview. Mike and Jimmy had decided to get along, while the rest of us — including the media — expected a big throw-down fight after the race. Was Jimmy upset with Mike for his moves on the racetrack? Absolutely! Was Mike angry over Jimmy's unwillingness to let him get by? Yes. But they both decided to just get along and call it a night.

The only thing a verbal or fistfight would have accomplished was a monetary fine and possible suspension from NASCAR. Now, I would be lying if I said I don't enjoy a little heated battle between drivers every once in a while. Any race fan would. But sometimes, to make your life a little easier you just have to learn to get along and realize you're not always right. And by the way ... Jimmy Spencer is still on my Christmas card list.

TONY
STEWART

"SET YOUR SIGHTS"

...

When you are asked to describe Tony Stewart in NASCAR, the nickname "NASCAR's Bad Boy" comes to the top of your mind, because that's what the media focused on a couple of years ago. Yes, Tony has displayed some temper-related incidents in his racing career, but it's what most drivers have felt every weekend. Tony just doesn't hide emotion. When you ask me to describe Tony Stewart, I would say he is a focused and dedicated driver and probably the most serious racer in the NASCAR Winston Cup garage. Racing is what flows through Tony's veins, and just racing five hundred miles every Sunday isn't enough. Tony will race anything and enjoys every lap he takes on. After you read his life lesson, you may understand his drive a little more and realize how dreams are realized.

On a cold Indiana winter morning, an amateur racer blew through a road-blocking snowdrift to arrive on time for work. In Rushville, Indiana, a machine shop sat in the middle of an open field. Tony Stewart would arrive early each morning to sit on a metal stool with a small space heater to fight off the frigid chill and earn five dollars an hour working as a machinist with no formal training. This one morning was different for Stewart. He was about to make a life changing decision, one on which he would set his sights to accomplish and never look back.

Tony grew up dreaming about racing Indy cars. Most kids growing up in Indiana had the same dream, but this racer took it the extra step.

"Every day after school in May, at 25 minutes after three o-clock, I would run home and turn on the TV to see racing updates. I wanted to see who ran the fastest, who crashed. I wanted to see what was going on at the speedway all the time."

Racing part time on the weekends kept Tony away from high school parties or hanging out with buddies. He didn't drink, he didn't smoke, he just raced. When everyone graduated from high school, most of Tony's friends went to college, but Stewart had no aspirations to attend a university or learn a vocational trade. He moved to Rushville to live with a family that helped him race quarter midgets.

This one Monday, Stewart had just returned from the Phoenix Copper Classic. This was one of the biggest and first USAC Midget races of the season. Tony ran second in the USAC Silver Crown race. The car made $8,600 that day, and Tony's portion of the prize money totaled $3,500. As he sat shivering, making the same machine parts all day long, an idea came to mind.

"I thought about how many hours I would have to work making five dollars an hour to collect a $3,500 paycheck. Maybe instead of only racing two days a week, I could race four and quit this job and race for a living."

Prior to that Monday morning, Stewart was forced to miss certain races in Wisconsin or events run on Sunday nights due to being at work on time each week. After an afternoon of thinking out his idea, Tony returned home to talk to the family he was living with.

"I told them I was turning in my two-weeks notice, and they immediately told me I shouldn't do it."

Knowing the ups and downs of a single race, they discouraged Tony's plan, telling him not every race would pay like the Copper Classic, but Tony felt differently. He felt he needed to try, and he truly believed he could make it work.

"That was the one life-changing decision I made in my life. From that moment on, there were times that life was harder than in my days at the machine shop, but at the same time, I was working toward a goal that got me into Winston Cup racing. You start at the bottom and work your way up. The people who work the hardest and are the most dedicated to what they are doing are the ones who get to the top."

Working odd jobs at car washes, driving a wrecker, sealing parking lots in the middle of the night, and even working as a maintenance man at a hotel kept Tony racing every week. Some weeks it took borrowing money from trusting friends to pay the entry fee at a track. Working at McDonalds was Tony's best job, since he could work a flexible 40 hours in a week and still race.

"There were many nights that I'd sleep in my car at the racetrack. We'd sell T-shirts in the pits and I would store the shirts in Tupperware containers in my Mazda RX7. At night, I would unload the car of the T-shirt containers and my gear, and then make a bed and pillows out of the T-shirts using plastic bags as a liner. In order to fit in my car, I would sleep with my head in the hatchback of the car and my feet resting on the gear shift. Even in the roughest of times, I enjoyed what I was doing."

In 1995, Tony Stewart arrived at the Indy 500 wearing an A.J. Foyt team uniform. Eddie Cheaver was driving, and Tony was working on the pit crew. His day ended eight seconds into the race when Stan Fox and Cheaver collided.

"I was so excited in 1995, just to say that I worked on a pit crew and got to wear an A.J. Foyt Enterprises uniform. If I had to give anyone advice, I'd say to set your sights on a goal. Surround yourself with people who will help you in your goal and do whatever it takes to accomplish it."

One year later, Stewart returned to the Indy 500. This time he was the driver, and he had the pole.

Larry McReynolds (left), Ernie Irvan and Robert Yates (right) celebrate one of their many wins together.

Martha Nemechek is a fixture on the NASCAR Winston Cup Series circuit, and there's no question she's son Joe's biggest fan.

(Top) After retiring as a driver, Benny Parsons took to broadcasting naturally. His outgoing personality and credentials as a former champion provide easy access to the sport's stars such as Bill Elliott.

(Bottom) During his career, Benny Parsons had the opportunity to work with some of the best minds the sport had to offer, including legendary crew chief Harry Hyde.

(Top) Mike Skinner claims a Japanese victory as a rookie in 1997.
(Bottom) Here I am with Mike prior to the Brickyard 400 in 2003. Another hurdle cleared and
a new ride to take on in the #01 Army car.

This was our engagement shot. It was taken before the spring Talladega race in 2000. Mike finished second, and I got my engagement ring the next day!

(Top) Mike Skinner (4) and Jimmy Spencer vie for the same real estate alongside Jeff Burton (99) during the 2003 Winston Open at Lowe's Motor Speedway.
(Bottom) Although he's known as a fierce competitor on the track, "Mr. Excitement" knows that's where the battles belong.

Tony Stewart has his sights set on being the best he can be. When that means beating everyone else out on the track, Stewart doesn't mind celebrating in style!

Tony Stewart celebrates his 2002 NASCAR Winston Cup Series championship with crew chief Greg Zipadelli.

Kenny Wallace flashes his trademark smile.

1989 NASCAR Winston Cup Champion Rusty Wallace is still a favorite among fans at every stop on the NASCAR Winston Cup Series tour.

Darrell Waltrip celebrates his win in the inaugural The Winston with wife Stevie by his side.

(Top) Quiet confidence turned into unbridled enthusiasm when Michael Waltrip broke into the winner's column in the 2001 Daytona 500.
(Bottom) Michael Waltrip and wife Buffy pose with the winner's trophy after the 2003 Pepsi 400 at Daytona.

Humpy Wheeler's positive attitude was instrumental in overcoming many challenges along his road to success.

Leonard Wood has been involved in NASCAR Winston Cup racing as a driver and team owner for more than 50 years. Below, he discusses the sport's modern-day challenges with longtime colleague Richard Petty.

Robert Yates and Davey Allison plot race strategy in the garage at New Hampshire in 1993. Yates gives much credit to Allison for encouraging him to purchase the race team and form Robert Yates Racing.

KENNY
WALLACE

"MIXED EMOTIONS"

...

People love NASCAR Winston Cup Series driver Kenny Wallace. His contagious laugh and fun-loving antics have made him one of the most likeable drivers in the garage area. Most people strive to be accepted for their personality, but for Wallace, his charismatic appeal forced him to make one of the hardest decisions in his career.

At the age of 22, Kenny Wallace began a mission to be one of the world's top stock car drivers. He grew up in a racing family in St. Louis. With his two older brothers, his father, and even his uncle already competing in the sport, this younger sibling decided it was his turn. Wallace got a late start, but that didn't stop his drive to be taken as a serious competitor.

Wallace started his career in 1982 with a win in the Street Stock State Championship in Illinois. He followed up as a weekly threat in the ASA ranks, winning races and Rookie of the Year honors in 1986. By 1989, Wallace gained his spot in NASCAR Busch Series competition as driver for brother Rusty's newly formed operation. In his first three years of NASCAR Busch Series competition, Kenny captured two wins. Wallace moved onto Team SABCO racing in 1992, and again won in that season. 1993 saw Kenny moving up to the NASCAR Winston Cup Series with Team SABCO in search of rookie accolades, but success was not found, and Wallace left the organization at seasons' end, which brings us to the year 1994.

In that year, Wallace received a phone call that caught him off guard. He had returned to the NASCAR Busch Series with FILMAR racing. The team was good and Kenny was winning, but the fans thrived to see Kenny doing something else.

"I got a phone call from TNN. They were covering races along with ESPN at the time. They wanted me in the broadcast booth as a color commentator. I had been making some television appearances over the years just for fun. At first, I thought it sounded like a fun thing to do because I wasn't racing on Sundays in Winston Cup anyway, but I didn't know if I was ready to give up on my racing career."

Not only did TNN want to hire Kenny, but the race fans also desired to see more of the driver that made them laugh.

"I was doing a lot of appearances and autograph sessions at this time and began to have hundreds of people come up and say, 'Congratulations on winning that Busch race, but we sure would like to see you in the booth.' I even had some say that I needed to get out my race car and get into the broadcast booth."

Even though the comments were compliments, they made Kenny angry. He took the suggestions from his fans the wrong way and went to his brother, Rusty, for some advice.

"All the comments started really bothering me. I told Rusty, 'Man, people want me to get in that TV booth and I don't want to do that. I'm a racecar driver!' Rusty explained to me that I was thinking wrong. He went on to tell me that being on television was a good thing and asked me if I felt it helped my racing career."

That advice led Kenny to look at his television offers in a new light. He learned a lot about marketing and creating an image for himself. Soon, he saw more drivers start to become part-time pit reporters. Even brother Rusty began hosting a racing show. As a result, Kenny learned how to deal with people saying they would like to see him in the booth, but he still wanted to be considered a hard-core racer, not a jokester that did a great job on television.

Wallace's racing career still went forward. He re-joined the NASCAR Winston Cup Series in 1995, but saw dismal results. Kenny knew he needed to get with a competitive organization to display his true talent in driving a racecar. He also had a goal to win a NASCAR Winston Cup race. By the middle of 2000, Kenny was once again faced with a major dilemma: to race or join the broadcasters in the booth. This time the offer was large. NASCAR had just signed multi-year contracts with primetime networks FOX and NBC. The president of FOX Sports called Kenny.

"I will never forget that phone call. I was on my cell phone making circles around my swimming pool. He told me a story about football great Howie Long. Long quit his career with the Oakland Raiders early for a career in television. He explained to me that I was a good racecar driver, but I could really parlay a TV career into something even bigger."

Once again, Kenny was upset over an incredible opportunity, but his feelings remained strong about staying a driver. That decision became final after Kenny visited an old friend for advice. Larry Philips was a racing legend in the Midwest. He won numerous NASCAR championships in the Late Model division, and Kenny grew up admiring his talent.

"I went to visit Larry in Springfield, Illinois. I told him about the opportunity with FOX, and I told him that I still loved to race. He looked me square in the eyes and said, 'You can't do that, you're a racer.' It made me feel so good. I looked back at him and said, 'You are right!'"

That was the end of the topic; Kenny knew he couldn't give up on his dream until he was done with it. He called up the FOX Sports president and told him of his decision.

Later that same year, Wallace found himself in another team transition. He left Andy Petree Racing for a new opportunity with a start-up team, Eel River Racing.

"I thought switching teams would help me toward my goal to win a Winston Cup race, but I made a mistake. They didn't have a sponsor and we were not quite halfway through the season in 2001. Then I get another phone call. This time it was Benny Parsons." Benny had been named as one of the main announcers for NBC's broadcasts that would take place beginning mid-season. Wallace was taking in one of his daughter's softball games when his cell phone rang.

"Benny said it looked like the FOX announcers were having an awful fun time calling the races with three men in the booth. NBC only had two men; they felt a third would make the show more complete and wanted me to audition for the position."

Repeating the past, Kenny explained that he really wasn't interested in ending his driving career just yet. Then Benny reminded Wallace that his NASCAR Winston Cup team was falling apart without a sponsor. Even though Kenny was running a NASCAR Busch Series car, Benny felt he should not pass up a tryout. Kenny agreed to Benny's offer but only after seeking more advice from those he admired.

"During the Charlotte race in May, I went to fellow driver Kenny Schrader to get his opinion. He suggested I discuss the matter with car owner Richard Childress. Richard had been in the business for a long time, and I felt he would give good advice. He told me I was a good driver but maybe joining the NBC broadcast for the end of the year and not signing a long contract couldn't hurt."

Richard's advice gave Kenny some confidence, and he showed up for the audition with a pretty carefree attitude.

"Well hell, I thought it was no big thing, but they flew in executives from New York wearing trench coats and carrying their brief cases. I started thinking, 'Man, what have I got myself into?' To me, the audition was just something fun to do and a way to make sure I clicked with the other guys in the booth. It was a full blown audition."

Wallace was caught off guard, but he still put on a great show. Along with Allen Bestwick and Benny Parsons, Kenny fake-called a night race previously run in Richmond. Kenny was actually a driver in the race and had some fun calling his own moves in the event. He had a pretty good time and walked away from the experience with a good feeling. Then he turned his cell phone on. While he was auditioning for NBC, his NASCAR Winston Cup team was frantically trying to find him. There were seven messages on his voice mail. Eel River Racing found a sponsor for the remainder of the year. It was a no-brainer for Kenny; he would remain a racer once again.

Most people would say he made a mistake because Eel River ended up shutting down before the year even ended, but the misfortune actually opened up a door for Wallace's racing career. NASCAR Winston Cup driver Steve Park had been injured in an accident in September at Darlington. Dale Earnhardt Inc. needed a replacement while Steve recovered from his injuries, and they called Kenny. Now he had a chance to show is ability as a hard-core racer. Dale Earnhardt Inc. had some of the series' most competitive cars, and Kenny knew this was his chance to shine. Kenny ended his season on a high note with a NASCAR Busch Series win, pole positions in both Busch and Cup and, most importantly, solid finishes in the NASCAR Winston Cup series. His performance with Dale Earnhardt Inc. provided him a full-time offer with Bill Davis Racing to run in the NASCAR Winston Cup Series in 2003.

"You never know what opportunity is around the corner. If I would had taken that NBC job and Steve Park got hurt, I would have never been able to get in that car on Sunday and show my ability and propel myself into the Bill Davis Racing ride. I learned a big lesson: never give up on what you are trying to accomplish because other people think that's what you should do. You have to run your course."

I agree with Kenny. When things aren't going well, people want to pile on and suppress your drive to win. They tell you that maybe you need to move onto something new, but you can't take their advice unless you know in your heart that you are ready. Second guessing your decisions can drive you crazy. Kenny knew he had not seen the right situation with the right team. He's hoping his chance is near with Bill Davis Racing.

"Don't give up on what you want to do. Don't sell yourself short. I didn't learn this right away, it took me from 1994 to 2001 to be comfortable with my decision. I'd be sick at my stomach sitting in that booth on Sunday knowing that I could still drive."

It doesn't mean Kenny doesn't want to be calling races for the networks one day, but his chance came a little too early. Now, I have to admit, hearing Kenny's laughter would be a plus to the race broadcast, but Kenny Wallace just isn't ready to stop driving.

RUSTY
WALLACE

"BONUS POINTS"

...

When I sat down with 1989 NASCAR Winston Cup Series Champion Rusty Wallace, he was quick to tell me his most important turning point was when he finally sat down and chose quality over quantity. Racing every weekend and spending his off days on the road to make personal appearances and meet with sponsors created havoc in his life and made him crave a normal family life – at least whatever normal family life one of NASCAR's most popular drivers could have.

"I was out racing every week and doing the best I possibly could. Finally I sat down one day and said, 'If I can manage all this stuff right, I could possibly start having a normal life.'"

Rusty's answer to his dilemma was to invest in aviation. He not only bought an airplane, he also became a certified pilot. Private aviation brought some calmness to Rusty's busy schedule by giving him more time at home. He could control his travel plans around his schedule and not be dependent on the airlines. Without a private airplane, Rusty would usually have to leave home on Wednesday to get to the next race, and then have to wait until Monday to get a flight home. By flying himself, Rusty improved his time spent at home by almost three days per week.

"I spent a lot of money on aviation, and that started getting my family life back in order. The amount of time I could spend at home was better. Then I just told myself that I would start spending my time concentrating on quality instead of quantity. Once I set my sights on quality, my productivity stepped up."

Improving his family life with quality made this racing star content, but, ironically, a goal toward quantity of points won Rusty his sole championship.

In 1988, Rusty Wallace lost the NASCAR Winston Cup Series championship to Bill Elliott by only 24 points. Being a fierce competitor, Rusty was bothered by the slim margin, but, being a professional, he went to New York for the year-end awards banquet and enjoyed his second-place standing in the series. After the trophies and awards were handed out, Rusty could not forget about losing the championship, and in the weeks following the awards banquet, he sat down and started looking over his season's stats.

"When it was all said and done, I said to myself, 'Man, I drove my guts out and I did all I possibly could and I still lost. How did I do that?'"

The answer soon dawned on him. He realized he never placed much importance on leading laps. In the NASCAR Winston Cup Series, you earn five bonus points if you lead one lap in a race. If you lead the most laps, you earn another five points. Most racers and crews call this "points racing," and many teams do anything they can strategically just to get those additional five points each race.

"I could not believe I had let that many points lay. It never crossed my mind because all I ever heard was to take care of my equipment and race when I needed to race. Don't race hard all of the time, only race when you need to race. There's a big difference between someone who can run fast and someone who can win. I had to understand that."

The downfall of trying to lead so many laps was the possibility of tearing up the equipment while trying to get to the front. In 1988, the cars were not as durable as they are today. You could win a short race by being aggressive, but it was very hard to win a long race with an aggressive style. With that in mind, Rusty started concentrating on a strategy to accumulate the maximum amount of points in each race.

"I thought to myself, 'Man, if I would have just gone out there and led three or four more times, I would have won the championship.'"

At that point, in December 1988, Wallace set a personal goal for his 1989 season: He would go out and try to lead a lap in every race. Rusty told himself that if he could lead the most laps, then go for it, but if he couldn't, then try for one per race. Get every bonus point he could. If Wallace could lead one lap per race, it would contribute 125 bonus points toward the championship.

Rusty Wallace had set a goal for quantity in points; it brought him much more.

Wallace scored six victories, seven pole positions and ended up with 120 additional bonus points at the end of his season. When it was all said and done, Wallace drove into victory lane after the last race of the year and celebrated the NASCAR Winston Cup Series championship, won by 12 points over Dale Earnhardt. Once again, a slim margin determined the title, but this time, Rusty Wallace would sit at the head table at the awards banquet in New York City.

"I still look back at that goal I set in December 1988. If I hadn't gone into that season with that goal, I wouldn't have won. There's no way. That was only 12 points – like leading only three times."

Those little bonus points made all the difference in Rusty's career. He can say he's a NASCAR Winston Cup Series champion. Rusty will still tell you that quality usually overrides quantity, but sometimes, the little things still add up.

DARRELL
WALTRIP

"DON'T BEAT YOURSELF UP!"

...

I truly feel the hardest life lessons are the ones where you have to lose to learn. Maybe that's because I am very hard headed and want things my way. But in reality, aren't we all? Maybe it's how we cope with our emotions that can change a disaster into success. Maybe after reading this story you won't feel as bad about your most recent life mishap, and hopefully, you might avoid a lose-and-learn lesson altogether.

In 1979, Darrell Waltrip was having the year of his life. He was winning races and leading the NASCAR Winston Cup points championship. He had a mission to de-throne "The King" Richard Petty and become the new king of NASCAR.

"My goal was to be the best there was, that had ever been in this sport. The way I would prove that was by beating Petty, David Pearson, Cale Yarborough and Bobby Allison. In 1979 I had my chance."

Equipped with a solid race team, including Buddy Parrot and Gary Nelson, race engines by Robert Yates and a secure sponsorship with Gatorade to pay the bills, Waltrip started the season off with a second-place finish in the Daytona 500. This was the famous race when Cale Yarborough and Donnie Allison fought in turn three after wrecking one another near the end. CBS was televising the whole display, and Waltrip eased into a top finish with the entire world watching two veteran drivers duking it out and a young aggressive driver approaching his prime. Richard Petty won the race, Waltrip finished second and A.J. Foyt third. That fueled the fire for "DW" and before he knew it, the Gatorade team had won seven NASCAR Winston Cup races and had a 300-point lead on the NASCAR Winston Cup championship.

"They were already engraving the trophy and writing the checks. There was no doubt in our minds that we would win the championship. It was September and there were only a few races left, but then the Southern 500 changed things drastically."

This particular weekend brought a fill-in driver for Dale Earnhardt, who had to recover from a wreck at Pocono. The Wrangler team chose the best fill-in available, Mr. Darlington himself, David Pearson. The Southern 500 was a race Darrell loved. He looked at this event as part of the NASCAR Triple Crown. If you won the Daytona 500, the Charlotte World 600 and the Southern 500 in Darlington, then you'd elevate yourself into a high racing status - and he wanted to be the new king. With Pearson filling in for Earnhardt, the race took on even more appeal for Waltrip.

"I felt this particular race could be a double. Not only could I go out and beat Petty, I would get the chance to beat Pearson, the guy all considered to be the 'King of Darlington.' He had more wins than anyone else: 11 total. He owned this joint."

Waltrip started the race with a real hot rod. With the fastest car in the field, he literally had lapped just about everyone on the track.

"In the seventies and eighties, it wasn't uncommon for the second-place car to sometimes be a couple laps down. The good cars would just lap all the others. I had lapped everyone except David Pearson. I remember thinking that I had a lap on the field and Pearson was the only one I hadn't lapped. I started driving like a maniac."

With only 50 laps to go, crew chief Buddy Parrot became nervous. He knew his driver had the race won, but he also knew that was not the only goal for DW that afternoon.

"I just knew I could achieve a huge accomplishment putting Pearson a lap down. I finally caught him and acquired the pass. That's when Buddy Parrot and my crew came on the radio pleading for me to slow down."

Buddy reassured Waltrip that he had the race won; all he had to do was just cruise to the finish. The driver responded with, "Shut up! Leave me alone. I know what I am doing!"

Getting closer to the finish, DW decided to look back and see just how far he had left Pearson behind. Before he knew it, the "Lady in Black" took a bite out of his racecar. "I went a little high into the loose stuff and ended up in the fence. With a lap lead on the field and only 20 to go until the checkered flag, I hit the fence. Spinning down into the first turn, I cranked it back up. It was wounded and all out of whack, but we were still on the lead lap. I went into the pits for fresh tires, but the front end was all knocked out, and I ended up hitting the wall again. I don't even know where I finished."

The crew and driver left the Southern 500 with controversy. The team fell apart. They were mad at DW and could not put the race behind them. They would not forgive their driver's mistake, and Darrell knew it. The steam was lost, and before DW knew it, there were only two races left in the season. Richard Petty had caught Waltrip in the championship battle. They entered the last race of the year in Ontario, California, with only a two-point lead. They didn't have a good day.

"The older guys like Petty and Buddy Baker were good buddies; they'd make deals before races. This Sunday, Buddy Baker was on the pole. He agreed to allow Petty an opportunity to lead and achieve five bonus points in the championship standings."

With a three-point advantage over Waltrip, Petty was now in the lead, but then there was a caution. Everyone pitted except Waltrip and his Gatorade team; they stayed out to lead a lap and get their points lead back. The smart decision put DW back on top, but it also put him at the back of the pack for the restart. As he approached the back straightaway, a three-car accident developed. Waltrip spun to avoid the mess. He didn't hit a thing but needed to come in the pits for fresh tires.

"My crew told me to pit, but they brought me in too early. While the tires were being changed on pit road, I got lapped. Now we were a lap down, and Richard Petty is running third. He ended up finishing the race third as well, and I finished sixth or seventh. But in the championship, he beat me by only eleven points. I was devastated. The whole latter part of the year, I just couldn't believe I'd done it to myself. I had the best car, the best team, and the chance of a lifetime to win a championship, and I just let it all slip away because of my own ignorance. I knew Richard had to be laughing; he probably loved me. He didn't have to beat me, I beat myself."

Waltrip went on to a new team owned by Junior Johnson and finally won that championship – three to be exact. But it was Johnson who taught Waltrip how to race for a championship.

"As I look back at the difference, Junior just didn't allow us to beat ourselves. He made sure you kept composed and under control; he didn't let you get in a position to beat yourself. I realized I didn't have to prove anything anymore, so I could then start being smart and let others beat themselves."

Racecar drivers, like all of us, always want to do better. If you win one race, then you want to win five more. If you win a championship, then you want to have the most championships. The phrase "you have to lose one to win one" can apply to all of us, but what if you changed your outlook to: you need the experience to know how to win one?

MICHAEL
WALTRIP

"QUIET CONFIDENCE"

. . .

By the 2001 Daytona 500, Michael Waltrip had started 462 NASCAR Winston Cup Series races. He had no official victories. The media, the race fans and the competitors all wanted to dwell on his winless record, but Waltrip wouldn't buy into the hype. He believed he was good enough to take the checkered flag first. He believed he would not only win just one, but many races before he would call it quits. He did win the Daytona 500 that February afternoon in 2001. He won the "500" again in 2003. He proved the critics wrong, and he proved he had the confidence in himself to never called it quits.

"My career is the perfect example of don't ever give up. It's human nature for people to talk about the negative, but I never would buy into that story. I didn't think it was fair to be judged as a loser, so I never gave up."

Waltrip calls his confidence "quiet confidence," knowing inside that you have the skill, but not bragging about your abilities. It is understanding that it's your responsibility to be all you can be and not buying into the negative comments made by other people. Michael had been a part of the NASCAR Winston Cup circuit for many years before his Dayton 500 victory. He never doubted his abilities, but he did do things to quietly prove to others that he could be a winner.

"It started out as simply just running. Kind of like the movie "Forest Gump;" one day I just started running."

The Friday after Thanksgiving in 1995 brought on Michael's new desire to run. Waltrip was preparing to drive for the Wood Brothers. Disgusted with his weight and feeling the need for a new goal, he looked at his pilot, Jon, and said, "Today we are going to start running!" They ran for 20 minutes that first day and set a goal to run a 10K race in one hour. Their goal needed to be reached in Charlotte by January.

"I would run around racetracks and I wanted people to know I would do whatever it took and whatever I could do in order to be the best racecar driver."

Waltrip then took his running to the next level and set a goal to run a marathon, mainly to prove to himself that he could do it and because he felt it would benefit his racing.

"While I was running, I'd think to myself, 'This is hard, but it's gonna make it a lot easier to run the Southern 500 at Darlington in September.'"

Michael's comparison was unique. He knew no other drivers were running marathons; he also knew that a marathon took about the same time to run as a NASCAR Winston Cup race. Waltrip would concentrate on racing while running.

"I could feel mentally unbeatable. When a race started I'd tell myself, 'They may outrun me on the racetrack, but they won't outlast me because I can run for 41/2 hours on my feet. I know I can sit on my butt and drive for 41/2 hours.'"

Waltrip still runs today, but not as much. His efforts to complete the marathon were mainly to prove to himself that he could do it. The repercussions were that other people saw he could conquer a dream and realized his determination to be a better racecar driver. The hard work and quiet confidence finally paid off.

In the late months of the 2000 NASCAR season, Waltrip caught the eye and attention of a life-long friend. Dale Earnhardt had faith in Michael's abilities and signed him to a contract with his organization, Dale Earnhardt Inc. Michael knew he had a good chance to win his first Cup race with such a competitive team, and in his first race with DEI, he proved victorious.

Michael Waltrip may had been written off as one of NASCAR's also-rans, but he showed the onlookers that he could not only win, but also win the most prestigious race, the Dayton 500, twice. Since then, he has also captured winning trophies for numerous NASCAR Busch Series races and continues to finish in the top 10 most weeks in the NASCAR Winston Cup Series.

"My whole point is, don't ever give up. Don't let other people make you out to be something you're not. If you're struggling, don't let them tell you that you can't win. Basically, just stay balanced and have quiet confidence."

H.A. "HUMPY"
WHEELER

"POSITIVE ATTITUDES"

. . .

If you have ever been to Lowe's Motor Speedway (formally named the Charlotte Motor Speedway) for any of the NASCAR Winston Cup Series races, then you know that the pre-race ceremony is just as spectacular as the actual race. The festivities and excitement are largely due to the speedway's president and general manager, Humpy Wheeler. He is the king of over-the-top promotions and known for putting the fans first at his racetrack. Racing is nothing new to this creative genius; he started promoting racing events right out of college at the age of 22.

"When I got out of the University of South Carolina in the early 1960s, I took over a little dirt track called Robinwood Speedway in Gastonia, North Carolina. I was out on my own and had no money, so I borrowed $3000 from the Bank of Belmont. It was all of the money I had."

With his small loan, Humpy got the track up and running, offering fans 2500 seats. They introduced a different kind of car to race that was cheap and simple. They had tremendous success, and if you didn't get to the track by 7 p.m., you would not get a seat. Humpy was not quite ready for so much so quickly and found himself developing a unique accounting system.

"I had a chest of drawers and was still living in my mother's house. In the top drawer was where I put my money, in the second drawer was where I put the bills. If I had more money in the top drawer than I had in the second drawer, then I figured I was making money."

The little dirt track ended up becoming too successful. Wheeler and his crew were not ready for the traffic backups and the nuisance it caused the community. They ended up having to close it down. Humpy continued on and ventured upon other tracks, while continuing to pack his chest of drawers with lots of profit. During that time period, Humpy found a part-time promoting position at Charlotte Motor Speedway. Though he ran additional tracks around the Carolinas, Charlotte Motor Speedway was his main source of guaranteed income. By 1963, Humpy Wheeler was only 25 years old and his inexperience had caught up with him.

"I ended up losing all the money I had earned and found myself married and with a young child. I also ended up getting fired from Charlotte Motor Speedway for something I never did figure out. So here I was with no source of income and no savings. I had lost everything."

With a family to keep up and a lot of anger toward losing his primary job, Humpy called an old friend for some advice. His friend didn't have a path for Humpy to follow and he didn't have a new job for Humpy to jump into; he had a new attitude for Humpy to live by.

"He simply said, 'Don't pour anymore energy into the negative, turn everything into a positive. Don't think about getting fired and only think that the next job you get is going to be a good one.' That one phone call changed the whole picture. I stopped being mad and started taking the energy from being angry and put it into being productive."

Two days after Humpy started thinking about the positive, he received a phone call from an important stockholder at Charlotte Motor Speedway. The organization was opening a road course in Augusta, Georgia. They had a 500-mile NASCAR race and needed a promoter fast. With literally no money, Humpy gathered his family and moved to Augusta for his new challenge.

"The race took place. Dave McDonald won and Fireball Roberts finished second. It was the first and last race they ever had."

Without a job once again, Humpy marched on toward another racing adventure, but this time, he had a new outlook on his ventures. When he returned to Charlotte from Augusta, a new opportunity was available. Firestone Tire Company had a job opening in their racing division and they wanted Humpy Wheeler to fill the position.

"For seven years I worked with Firestone. That is really where I got my masters degree in auto racing. I was introduced to Indy racing and Formula One. I got to see world speed records at the Bonneville Salt Flats and many other interesting projects. I got to see big-time racing from a different level, and it really helped me professionally."

Even though Humpy enjoyed his career with Firestone tremendously, his obstacles were far from over. The tire company abruptly decided to get out of racing after being involved in the sport since 1909. To add to the dismay, Humpy's father passed away and he caught a combination of the mumps and mononucleosis all within a month. Wheeler found himself wondering once again what to do with his life. He was only in his early thirties.

"It really worked on me because I was faced with starting over again and it was a tough time, but I remembered what that man had said to me about being positive instead of negative. It just helped."

After a lot of prayer and positive thinking, things did start to turn around. Humpy refused to be down and worked a few jobs in real estate. He also started another dirt track over a three-year period after the Firestone devastation.

Throughout this time period, Humpy did keep in touch with another business-man, O. Bruton Smith. Today, Bruton Smith owns and operates all the SMI (Speedway Motorsports Inc.) racetracks, among many other businesses. But Bruton, too, had been fired by a trustee of Charlotte Motor Speedway two years earlier than Humpy's dismissal. Years later, Bruton had managed to gain control of the racetrack that had let him go and he wanted Humpy to come back as well.

"The two guys that once were fired came back to Charlotte Motor Speedway. So now when anybody gets fired, I try to get to them. I always call and tell them this story. Getting fired is not the worst thing to ever happen to you. I actually think some of the best people in the business were fired one time or another."

In the fall of 1975, Humpy Wheeler returned to Charlotte Motor Speedway. He would promote all of its events. He is still there today and is known to be the best promoter in the racing business. Just turning the negative into the positive can help all of us in any situation. It may not fix your problem or offer a solution, but it can help you get over your grief and move to the next opportunity that life can provide.

"Life is messy at best, and its always got its challenges. No matter where you are, what you do, how little or much money you've got, you still have hurdles you've got to get through. You just have to keep jumping them, and you can't do it without that positive attitude."

LEONARD
WOOD

"ONE STEP AHEAD"

. . .

To be successful in stock car racing you have to be dedicated; you must have a passion for racing, and in order to be the best, you have to be one step ahead. It's common for the race teams that dominate in the NASCAR Winston Cup garage to have a secret no other race teams have discovered, or one that NASCAR officials haven't regulated. Maybe one team has figured out a better aerodynamics package or a gear ratio to make their motors run more efficiently. In the 1960s, the Wood Brothers got together and figured out their own way to get ahead of other race teams, and it was all in the pit stop.

Wood Brothers Racing was founded by Glen Wood who, along with his brother, Leonard, guided it to what it is today. It is the oldest continuously operating team in NASCAR history.

In 1960, the first World 600 took place at Charlotte Motor Speedway. At the time, Smokey Yunick was noted as one of the sport's great mechanics, and he had the legendary Fireball Roberts to drive his machines. Leonard Wood watched the fierce team during the competition and came back home to Virginia after the race with an observation.

"I remember watching their pit stops. It took them 48 seconds to change two tires and gas the car. I got to looking at it and thought, 'There's a lot to be gained in this stop.'"

The race teams were using four-pronged lug wrenches at that time, and Leonard racked his brain to come up with a device to make the stops faster. He knew if they could cut some time out of a pit stop, they could beat all the other teams off pit road and grant themselves a big lead. The Wood Brothers went to work right away.

"We got down to 25-second pit stops. We were using power wrenches."

After they discovered the efficiency of power wrenches, the brothers started to perfect their stops by synchronizing one another's' steps around the car. They even took the pit stop science one step further by installing springs in sockets to spit out lug nuts quicker. Then they fixed the jack.

"We were the first ones to speed up the jack. We figured out a way to lift the car in one stroke over the three it was taking at the time. The cars weighed 3800 pounds and the designers of the jack were so impressed that they filmed us jacking our race car in Michigan so they could build a better unit."

Right away, people started catching on to the speed of the Woods' pit stops. Their car was the first off pit road on a weekly basis, and their precision and ingenuity gave them a half-lap lead right out of the pits. They started winning a lot of races.

Other racing divisions also took notice, and in 1965, the Ford Motor Company asked the Wood Brothers to bring their creative crew to the Indianapolis 500 to pit a Scotsman's Indy car. The driver was Jim Clark.

"We went into the garage at Indianapolis not knowing if this European crew would accept us or resent our presence. They seemed to welcome us being there."

The brothers went to Indianapolis a week early to practice and secure their new fuel system. This would be the first time Indy cars would use gravity flow fuel instead of pressurized. When the team tested the new system, a USAC official made a smart comment.

"This official looked at us and shook his head, betting us $1000 that we would not be able to pour 20 gallons a minute out of our device. Well ... we weren't really concerned about proving to him how quick our device really was. We didn't want him to know how quick it was."

They tested their fuel system the day before the race. When they connected their hose and turned it on, it put out 58 gallons in a record 15 seconds. The critics figured they would be in the pits for over a minute, Leonard knew they would only need 20 seconds.

The race began, and the crew's first stop lasted only 17 seconds. The commentator at the Brickyard announced to the race fans that this new bunch in the pits was awfully green.

"The announcer said, 'You can bet they didn't get that fueled properly. They will have to come back into the pits in a few seconds, you can bet on that.'"

Minutes later he got back on the loudspeaker dismayed by the car's ability to remain on the race track. He claimed that the team must be running a mixture, which would only be half as much gasoline. Confused, he sent a pit reporter to ask the team owner what was in their fuel. The owner just said, "It's pure alcohol." Once again, the Wood Brothers were first with an invention to revolutionize pit stops. Jim Clark won that Indianapolis 500. The newspapers stated that his win came with better pit crewing, better refueling and better tires.

"It was one of those things where we got the most publicity in our lives. It went all over Europe because we all won the race. It was just funny to mix a Scottish guy and an English car owner with some Southern racers."

Today the Wood Brothers continue to compete for the NASCAR Winston Cup Series championship, and every weekend I can catch a glance of Leonard Wood still working in the pits, holding the pit sign to mark the driver's stopping point. I asked Leonard why they were first to revolutionize pit stops in NASCAR. His answer was pure dedication.

"You gotta really be dedicated and be interested in what you're doing. You have to want to do it. You have to love competition."

For Leonard, it's the thrill of competition and being the first one off pit road that makes him come back to the race track week after week, because it's a lot more fun to run up front than be in the back.

ROBERT
YATES

"THE POWER OF PEOPLE"

...

I f you say the word "engine" in the NASCAR Winston Cup garage, a specific person's name will always come up: Robert Yates. Yates has been producing horsepower for competition in the NASCAR Winston Cup garage since 1967 and developed two NASCAR Winston Cup teams that many racers strive to work for. How Yates developed such an honored reputation is a great story and one that began through many encouraging people — and all without a single plan.

Robert Yates grew up in a family with nine siblings in North Carolina. His father was a pastor, and the importance of education was emphasized. Robert became the odd man out in the family and rebelled against what was expected of him. He felt he didn't learn as well as the others in his family, but he did realize that he received a lot of praise when he worked on cars.

"My turning points came off of the people I ran into, starting with my sister."

Coming from a family who valued education, Robert's oldest sister decided to save her brother, who was skipping classes and receiving many speeding tickets from the police. The young racer would get his thrills from outrunning the North Carolina police. The police became tired of his antics and had his license suspended for one year with four years of restriction. With his passion for fast cars stripped away, he decided to go with his sister and brother-in-law to Wake Forest, N.C., to pursue his high school education. They were missionaries on the weekends and expected him study every weekday.

"My brother-in-law would unplug the television at 7 p.m. every night to make his children and me do our homework. After a while, I decided to study and, in my junior and senior years of high school, somehow made all 'A's. I was really street smart and realized I needed a formal education too."

Robert went on to college, but he still fell back on what he truly enjoyed doing: making cars go faster and faster. His education and passion for physics really paid off in 1967 when Homer Moody ran an ad in the newspaper for someone with math skills to work on his race team. Robert applied and, because he had some mechanical skills on top of his math abilities, received the job.

"I did every job that was given to me the best that I could do. A lot of times, I would take the worst job and do the best I could manage and get recognized from a manger."

Yates developed a passion for teaching compression ratios and also taught math to other engine builders in Moody's race shop. He went on to develop engines for the Wood Brothers and, in 1969, received his biggest break in racing.

"I put together the winning motor in the 1969 Daytona 500. Junior Johnson was the driver. I pulled all-nighters to build that engine, and the Monday after the race, Junior came into my shop and slipped me a one hundred dollar bill; that was big!"

In 1971, Junior Johnson rewarded the hard working engine builder by giving him a job in his race shop. With a wife and two young children in diapers, Robert built an engine shop beside Junior Johnson's facility. They spent long hours going through the pains of developing small-block motors and making their own pistons and rods. The hours soon became too much for Robert's wife, Carolyn, and the next major turning point in Robert's life came, again, from a loved one.

"Carolyn saw that I was getting nowhere with all the long hours spent in the engine shop. The sport was young and my family was starving. We had spent all of our savings and my family never saw me, even though the engine shop was next door to our home. She was always supportive of my love of building race engines, but she saw I wasn't getting the financial part of it, so she packed up with the kids and left. I followed her back home to Charlotte. Once again, my turning point came from someone coaching me to do better for myself."

Yates once again set up a race shop and built winning motors for seven teams. Pretty soon, some of the premiere race teams started recruiting Robert Yates for themselves. They saw the value of having the engine builder exclusively. Yates, along with his crew, acquired a winning reputation with DiGard and Darrell Waltrip. Using Yates' motors, Waltrip won 34 races and took 50 pole positions from 1976 to 1986. Needless to say, Robert was doing pretty well on his own until one opportunity became too good to turn down. In 1986, Ford Motor Company called Robert to think about a new team venture. Harry Ranier was going to start a new NASCAR Winston Cup operation. At the time, Ranier had no driver and no sponsor, but he knew he needed the horsepower of Robert Yates. Out of politeness, Yates agreed to give them a quick 30-minute meeting in a friend's office at a nearby private airport.

"I had no intention of accepting their offer. I looked outside the airport window and saw their jet land and two henchmen-like men walk off. We sat at a long conference table where the men laid out an unbelievable deal. We are talking I could buy a new house, cars, even cars for my kids with this offer. I looked at the men and told them I would have to sleep on it. They let me know that this was a deal that I could not sleep on. I would have to give them my answer before I walked out the door."

Knowing that the deal would be off the table if he walked out the door that afternoon, Robert decided to shake the men's hands and accept his new position. The deal was so good that Yates could even keep his own engine shop. In August 1986, Robert Yates went to work as a manager and engine builder for Ranier. Over a period of two years, the group captured Texaco as a sponsor and the great Davey Allison as their driver. The team built a lot of excitement and energy. Also over that two-year period, Yates discovered the race team was not as financially secure as presented in that conference room at the airport. The team was for sale.

It was at that point in Robert's life that another important person challenged him to bring on a new turning point. While Yates and Davey Allison sat on the pit wall at Charlotte Motor Speedway during a test session, Davey told Robert to buy the race team. Yates had never really longed to own a race team, but the sponsor was present, the driver was willing and there were 10 members of a team who wanted to continue their racing dreams.

"Davey looked at me and said, 'Why don't you buy the race team?' I looked back and asked if he was looking for a partner or something. He said, 'No, I think you should own your own race team; all I want to do is drive.'"

Robert immediately started brainstorming about possible financial partners he could use to make Davey's suggestion a reality, but Davey continued to encourage Robert that he didn't need anybody; he could do this on his own. Robert had saved some money from the success of his engine building business, but the team was for sale for $2 million. Yates talked them down to $1,704,000 but had a lot of things to sell before he could take ownership.

"I sold my house, my car, my engine shop and took out a loan. I moved my family into a little apartment and drove a $50 car and had the loan paid off one full year after Robert Yates Racing came into existence."

Robert Yates Racing started out on a sour note. They struggled, got in some crashes and even got rained out of a race when payroll was due. Robert was frustrated. He needed the purse money to pay his employees. Finally, in the fourth quarter of 1988, Davey finished second to Rusty Wallace in the last race of the year. It was a relief – and a start of great things to come for Robert Yates Racing.

"Life is a lot about who you have opportunities to associate yourself with. How people can help each other. I've never done anything on my own. I've gotten some great breaks and I'd like to think that I've given other people some breaks."

Davey Allison had enough faith in Robert to convince him to take the risk and buy a race team. Robert accepted the challenge, and he smiled as he noted that the legendary #28 team went on to help write some of the NASCAR Winston Cup recordbook. Yates feels you have to be challenged to be successful. I have to agree with him. Sometimes you don't know your full potential until someone reminds you or encourages you to go for it. Robert also reminded me that one person can't take all the credit. The best victory lane ceremony is the one where everyone celebrating contributed to the win.

"Those are just a few of my turning points. I had to get some formal education. I had to listen to my wife and leave a job when it wasn't headed toward where I needed to go, and I needed Davey Allison to jump up and say, 'Hey, go this way!'"

EPILOGUE

by ANGELA SKINNER

•••

Writing this book started out as a personal goal. I wanted to accomplish a feat that seemed hard to reach and fulfill my desire to achieve a task, which used my talent and ambition to be my own person. As a result, I learned a lot about life and discovered a few new ways to approach my emotions and aspirations.

It seems that we are all faced with some obstacle or desire to be a better person every day in our lives. Hearing or reading someone else's inspiring tale brings you that much closer to fulfilling your own needs and makes your own obstacle seem easier to overcome. Just knowing that you may have a sense of connectedness with other people or a shared experience makes you feel not so alone. In my case, the stories I heard from your favorite NASCAR celebrities inspired me and helped me overcome the hurdles that Mike and I face in the racing business. I also found a new respect for many of my friends in NASCAR and a lot of racing history. You turn on the news and hear so many negative reports about the evil or disturbed people in our world, but sometimes there is a feel-good story that makes you feel warm. That's what I hope I accomplished for you, the reader. We don't sit around on the back porch sharing tales of our good and bad fortunes anymore, but in the NASCAR garage, we still do, and that's one of the reasons why I love this sport.

Who knew so many NASCAR drivers were so philosophical? It just proves that everyone has a story to share and a turning point that proves we are all human. If every person who reads this book remembers just one chapter or life lesson, then I've accomplished my feat. If you apply that life lesson to your personal day-to-day life, then you've accomplished your own feat, and that's a turning point for you to share with many others.

Angela Skinner
August 2003

AUTOGRAPHS

AUTOGRAPHS

UMI Publications, Inc. publishes The Official NASCAR Preview and Press Guide. For subscription information, call 1-704-374-0420 or visit our website at www.umipub.com.